How Far to Nudge?

NEW HORIZONS IN PUBLIC POLICY

Series Editor: Wayne Parsons, *Professor of Public Policy, Wales Governance Centre, Cardiff University, UK*

This series aims to explore the major issues facing academics and practitioners working in the field of public policy at the dawn of a new millennium. It seeks to reflect on where public policy has been, in both theoretical and practical terms, and to prompt debate on where it is going. The series emphasizes the need to understand public policy in the context of international developments and global change. New Horizons in Public Policy publishes the latest research on the study of the policymaking process and public management, and presents original and critical thinking on the policy issues and problems facing modern and post-modern societies.

Titles in the series include:

How Far to Nudge?

Assessing Behavioural Public Policy

Peter John

Department of Political Economy, King's College London, UK

NEW HORIZONS IN PUBLIC POLICY

Cheltenham, UK • Northampton, MA, USA

Published by
Edward Elgar Publishing Limited
The Lypiatts
15 Lansdown Road
Cheltenham
Glos GL50 2JA
UK

Edward Elgar Publishing, Inc.
William Pratt House
9 Dewey Court
Northampton
Massachusetts 01060
USA

A catalogue record for this book
is available from the British Library

Library of Congress Control Number: 2017953165

This book is available electronically in the **Elgar**online
Social and Political Science subject collection
DOI 10.4337/9781786430557

ISBN 9781786430540 (cased)
ISBN 9781786430564 (paperback)
ISBN 9781786430557 (eBook)

Typeset by Columns Design XML Ltd, Reading
Printed and bound in the United States.
Printed on ECF recycled paper containing 30% Post Consumer Waste.

For Mike

Contents

Preface

Like many people, I drifted into nudge. In the 2000s, I was working on measures to encourage citizens to participate in politics and civic life. As someone interested in how to improve public policy outcomes, I had become intrigued about how to encourage citizens to do a wider range of acts for collective benefit. I wanted to motivate them with messages and acts of persuasion to overcome constraints on collective action (see John et al. 2011). In short, I discovered myself doing behavioural public policy at the same time as Thaler and Sunstein's (2008) book on nudge came out. I found the ideas and language of the behavioural sciences very helpful as I developed a research programme, especially as I was using randomised controlled trials, which is the method of choice for testing behavioural interventions.

I had of course long been aware of the strides of behavioural economics. I recall going to hear Danny Kahneman give a keynote lecture to the American Political Science Association in 1999. I had also worked with David Halpern on a project on social capital at the end of the 1990s. Anybody who talks to David cannot fail to be aware of his wide interest in the interactions between government policy and policy outcomes, which first manifested itself with his advocacy of the social capital agenda and then of behavioural insights. I kept in touch with David as he developed the behaviour change agenda in central government, and he has inspired me.

I also discovered that people working in public agencies found the skills I had developed in designing trials to be very useful in redesigning their policies. Some of these interventions were carried out with the Behavioural Insights Team (BIT) in its early days; latterly I worked with local authorities and other public agencies on their own behavioural insights. I became curious about the growing official interest in testing behavioural ideas with experiments, and I wondered how a culture of experimentation and behavioural redesign could be integrated into the standard operating procedures of public bureaucracies. I also became aware that I was one of the very few political scientists working on behavioural public policy. I had all the skills of the nudger and experimenter, but I saw the interventions much more in their political context. As a result, I wanted to understand how behavioural public policy could be useful to those who practised it. I was curious to find out why politicians are attracted to nudge and what bureaucrats value in the research and policy agenda. In short, I found that I had developed an interest in the politics of behavioural public policy and the factors that affected its diffusion and implementation. I believe that behaviour change reforms can only work effectively when considered as part of a wider system of institutions and interests, which involves understanding the mechanisms of accountability, citizen reactions, and private advantage. Nudging needs to operate within the current set of political constraints and opportunities, and these choices are best understood within a framework familiar to those who study political science and public policy. I developed many of these ideas while designing trials for behavioural public policy interventions and in thinking through their implications as I dealt day-to-day with bureaucrats and politicians. Doing behavioural public policy has inspired this book.

Acknowledgements

I have many people to thank. The first is Alex Pettifer at Edward Elgar. Like a good publisher, he knows the value of the long game. Alex and I had been meeting many times, long before the idea for the book was hatched. Once I had the project in mind, he helped me develop it, and I am very pleased this book is coming out under Edward Elgar's imprint. I am also very grateful to others at the press for helping me through the preparation of the manuscript, in particular Helen Moss and Kaitlin Gray.

I am in debt to many academic colleagues with whom I have developed behavioural interventions, in particular my co-researchers on the Rediscovering the Civic project – Sarah Cotterill, Hanhua Liu, Alice Moseley, Hisako Nomara, Liz Richardson, Graham Smith, Gerry Stoker, and Corinne Wales – for which we developed tests of both nudge and think (John et al. 2011). I also thank my friend Helen Margetts, with whom I have worked on nudge-like interventions in the online sphere. In the midst of writing our book on political turbulence (Margetts et al. 2016), I pitched her the idea of *How Far to Nudge?*, and she encouraged me to do it.

I am particularly grateful to members of the Behavioural Insights Team who welcomed me as a friend and advisor, especially in the early days. My special thanks go to David Halpern, Laura Haynes, Michael Sanders, and Owain Service. I am also grateful to my sister Ros who, as a professor of developmental epigenetics, advised me on the discussion of the role of epigenetics in affecting human behaviour in Chapter 2.

I appreciate the countless people with whom I have talked about behavioural interventions. Because of the trendiness of the topic, I have been invited to give many presentations to governments, third sector bodies, and academic gatherings. Of course, talking about one's ideas is the same as developing them and helping them take shape. These audience members listened patiently to my talks and asked very good questions at the end. I also presented ideas about behavioural public policy to the students who took my Making Policy Work course module, based on the eponymous book (John 2011), which I taught when I was in the School of Public Policy, University College London. Anyone reading the book will find out that I move inexorably from the tools of government to behaviour change, so the students knew instantly what direction I was taking them in. I claimed that I was planting favourable ideas about nudge and randomised controlled trials into the minds of the students, but in truth they influenced me just as much.

I also thank the School of Governance at the University of Utrecht, which invited me to spend a week there in November 2016, where I had quiet space to work, and I gave a talk based on the book's ideas. I thank Thomas Schillemans, who invited me, as well as Lars Tummers and Stephan Grimmelikhuijsen, who all made me feel very welcome. In the middle of the week, I discussed the ideas in the book over a delightful dinner with Joel Anderson, and he inspired me to develop them further.

I am very grateful to Oliver James, who reviewed the manuscript for the publisher critically and sympathetically. I thank the research students who work with me on behaviour change policies: Manu Savani, Annabelle Wittels, Eliza Kozman, and Patrick Taylor. We convened a mini-seminar on my book on 20 March 2017, which was great fun as well as offering me excellent feedback. Joel helped me once again with the chapter on ethics (Chapter 7). Sarah Birch, Oliver Hauser, Sebastian Jilke, and Gerry Stoker also made very useful comments on the manuscript after its first draft. Needless to say, I have probably made many mistakes by not listening enough to the great advice I have received.

1.   Introduction

We live in an age of large public policy problems that governments find hard to solve. These include obesity, climate change, terrorism, race discrimination, corruption, and youth unemployment, just to name a few current policy challenges. The list could go on to include a large number of other topics that range across all aspects of human experience. These problems share their origin in human behavioural traits or habits that persist over time. Behaviours create and sustain poor outcomes, both for individual citizens and communities, mainly because effective policy outcomes usually depend on some degree of citizen action and responsiveness. When citizens are engaged, motivated, and willing to change their behaviours, it is much easier for governments to achieve their policy objectives, partly because all citizens are joint participants in acts that have collective benefits. When citizens are switched off, antagonistic to governments, and focused on their short-term interests, public policy gets much harder to implement and poor outcomes are the result.

Whether helping or worsening policy outcomes, behaviours are often transmitted through peer groups and in close social networks. Behaviours get embedded, as they are reinforced through habit and mutual dependence. Even government policy has a role in sustaining behaviours that might be negative for the individual and society in spite of good intentions and many beneficial measures. In health, for example, the policy of responsive medicine and fixing problems immediately can undermine a more preventative approach based on promoting more healthy behaviours, as people expect to attend hospitals. As a result, the effort and resources of the public health services get concentrated on interventionist medicine. Many structural inequalities in income and capacity also influence human behaviour, which in turn reinforce existing inequalities. As many policies sustain these disparities, poor behaviours may continue over time, encouraged by governments as well as market forces. The implication of these factors is a negative equilibrium trap whereby collectively reinforced behaviours lead to poor outcomes. The trap occurs because it is rarely in the short-term interests of people, groups, economic enterprises, and even governments to change their behaviours, partly because of the potential cost each participant faces from moving from the current state of affairs to one where all benefit. The question that arises for policy-makers and social scientists is what measures and approaches could be used to create a step-shift in policy outcomes by reversing or changing embedded behaviours?

Governments or other public authorities are elected with a remit to try to solve public problems. They have a number of tools and considerable resources at their disposal to do so, whether taxes, laws, the capacity of their bureaucracies, or by being at the centre of networks of experts and sources of knowledge (Hood and Margetts 2007; John 2011). The challenge is to be able to use these tools effectively and efficiently change behaviours. The potential benefit of such official efforts is a sustained improvement in outcomes for society and the advancement of the common good. The deployment of human ingenuity and putting in place the right combination of resources might shift long-entrenched behaviours and lead to an upward movement in outcomes. Such a transformation often operates in a virtuous circle of self-reinforcing activities, such as a movement from a neighbourhood with high crime, low employment, low trust, and high degrees of social dysfunction to one where these attributes lessen over time and where positive actions emulate each other to sustain local economies, increase access to employment, and reduce anti-social activities.

Such entrenched behaviours, and corresponding opportunities, are often thought to characterise only poor communities, which do not have good opportunities for employment and are dependent on welfare. But richer communities can fail too, even those that have economic advantages and other opportunities but where not enough people contribute enough to social outcomes or innovate in the local economy, or where people become unwell from lack of exercise and unchecked affluent lifestyles.

Governments have tended to focus on solutions that come from the power of the state to change things, such as provide more units of public activities to address public problems directly, through increased public expenditure and employing greater numbers of public servants, such as police officers, nurses, and soldiers. As societies got wealthier and more settled they have been able to allocate resources and make regulations to ameliorate public problems. These solutions often depended on influencing individual actions, such as patients attending hospital clinics or the unemployed being ready for work; but changes to individual behaviour were not core to these programmes, which were about using the authoritative tools of the state to effect change.

In spite of the considerable successes of these initiatives, policy-makers and experts have come to realise that the use of such powers and resources often does not fully address the problems under consideration, mainly because they often cannot change the behavioural impulses and habits that sustain the problems over time. In part, many of the harms come from prosperity as people adopt more affluent lifestyles. In more complex societies, there are more interdependencies, which means that solving public problems entails tackling a range of human actions that interlock. Greater social science knowledge about the causes of public problems shows them to reflect these complexities and to depend on a range of reinforcing behaviours and actions.

To an extent, governments have always been aware of the need to change behaviour, whether it was asking people to volunteer, for example to serve in the armed forces, or advising them to take precautions against the spread of diseases, or ensuring they respond to new tax breaks or increases. People or organisations receive incentives from government, but to communicate these policies governments have often relied on simple pleas, as in posters and media campaigns, and the more gradual processes of education and information provision, as well as providing clear benefits and costs for desirable and non-desirable public actions (Becker 1968). In societies with high degrees of social deference and respect of authority, it is possible for a fully paternalist approach to work well. By communicating injunctions to change behaviour, backed up by laws and incentives, governments can create the changes in outcomes that are needed. It is possible to think of encouragements to eat healthily or to volunteer or to report crime as obvious tasks of government, but they depend on a respect for authority and expertise to work well. In today's society, such deference to government and experts has weakened; it has been replaced by a belief in consumer sovereignty and the right to have one's own opinions as to the good life, which is the natural end point of the liberal ideal. Expertise is often questioned and not trusted, which may be a result of increasing polarisation of issues and attitudes. Commonly-used measures based on incentives, command, or education may not change behaviour in ways they once did or appeared to do. People even resist commands because of the way in which they are put, as they do not like being told what to do or how to behave. Then there is information overload from multiple media sources, including social media.

If conventional methods of achieving change are not so efficacious, it is not surprising that governments tend to act on the consequences of the behaviours, putting right the effects rather than the causes of the problems. They adopt policies that help them get elected, such as providing more expenditure on hospitals or roads. It might be the case that providing more policy outputs is the most feasible course of action and the one that is politically the most possible. But many policy-makers want to make more of a difference. They know about limits to resources and they wish to find whether new ideas and knowledge can work. There is a common image of policy-makers operating according to a crude version of the rational actor model, in seeking votes or expanding their bureaus; but political action is more complex, and incorporates a public service motivation to do good for society (Ritz et al. 2016), which is one of the reasons people go into politics or public service in the first place. With an awareness of the limitations of the tools of government and a willingness to try new things out, the question becomes whether governments can address behaviour change head on with theories and approaches that speak to the behaviours themselves and change them.

BEHAVIOUR CHANGE AND NUDGE

The point about measures to address behaviour change is that they need to be based on theories about why the desirable behaviours are not occurring and then interventions that address those behaviours and change them. Better understandings of the drivers of behaviours and what causes changes in individual actions have the potential to transform public policies to ensure interventions and public decisions directly address fundamental problems of society. A powerful and growing movement in the social sciences has gathered pace in recent years with its radical agenda and scientific backing. Over the last three decades or so, the behavioural sciences and behavioural economics have incorporated insights from psychology about what motivates people to change their behaviour, ideas that have taken root in more established research programmes in economics and the policy sciences and have diffused to subject disciplines, such as studies of health and education. There has emerged an extensive research programme, which rigorously tests its claims, increasingly done through field experiments. It complements older traditions of research that use psychology to inform public policy, such as in health psychology, with the difference that the behavioural sciences are genuinely interdisciplinary and have a high level of public visibility and acceptability, so that they can reach into all aspects of public policy.

Out of studies of behavioural economics and behavioural sciences has come the greater interest by public agencies in using these ideas. This policy field is often called 'nudge' (Thaler and Sunstein 2008), which is often thought to be the idea that low-cost small changes, attuned to human psychology, can make large improvements to public policies, largely from encouraging citizens to do things that they would upon reasonable reflection agree with. Policy-makers of all different types have used theories and evidence on behaviour change in developing interventions, often helped by nudge units, such as the UK's Behavioural Insights Team (BIT) and the White House's Social and Behavioral Sciences Team. As a proof of concept, they deploy randomised controlled trials (Haynes et al. 2012), which randomise the message or nudge to an intervention or a control or non-intervention group, comparing outcomes, such as payment rates, between the groups. This procedure reaches a high standard of evidence in attributing a causal relationship between the nudge and the intervention (Gerber and Green 2012). It also creates headline results that are easy to interpret as percentage point differences, which can translate into benefits to the agency, such as increased revenue. This combination between respectability in methods, easy-to-understand headline results, and information for cost and benefit decisions has helped assist the dissemination of behavioural insights, within and across governments.

Armed with evidence from trials, agencies have been redesigning the messages that they send, such as telling taxpayers who are behind paying that nine out of ten others have already paid their bills, so conveying the social norm (Hallsworth et al. 2017), or making text messages more personal so people settle their court fines on time (Haynes et al. 2013). Influenced by the high level of official interest, academics of all types working in behavioural science now consider more policy-relevant applications of their research (Oliver 2013a; Shafir 2013), which also feeds back into the design of policy interventions. A large research agenda has been created on what is sometimes called behavioural public policy (Oliver 2017).

The nudge agenda has been assisted by skilful advocacy by academics and entrepreneurs, so its terms and understandings have entered the mainstream of debate and public policy. Such acts of dissemination have created the world of nudge and applied behavioural insights. Advocates, such as academics and heads of nudge units, have presented behavioural insights in a way that is pragmatic, apparently based on common sense, closely linked to the concerns of bureaucracies and responsive to their demands, in particular by addressing cost pressures. Partly as a result of this translation and diffusion, and the essential pragmatism of the enterprise, there has been an extraordinary success story in the use of behavioural insights. The result is that governments and other public agencies from a large number of jurisdictions have adopted a set of techniques that allow them to address key problems in public policy and improve the efficiency of public administration.

There are two dimensions of policies or procedures that need to be adjusted by the policy-maker: one is the communication flow to the citizen, which is based on a plausible psychological mechanism to change behaviour, such as peer pressure, norms, or availability; the other, in tandem with the first dimension, is an institutional change, an alteration of standard operating procedures, what Thaler and Sunstein (2008) call 'choice architectures', which are the rules and routines of public agencies that intersect and structure the choices of citizens and other actors, such as by offering defaults, opportunities, or new ways of doing business. The first dimension is what most people associate with nudge, for example the messages sent by BIT mentioned above. But it is the changes to institutional design that are core to behavioural public policy and are the sources of its agenda for a change in the delivery of public services. Otherwise nudge just becomes another version of what is called 'social marketing' (see discussion by Hallsworth and Sanders 2016, and in Chapter 3). In other words, to be more than the science of messaging, nudge involves a reform of political institutions and bureaucracies. As a consequence, nudge advocates propose changes in how public organisations operate internally as well as about how well they communicate with citizens. Partly as a result, the agenda of nudge integrates closely with core questions in political science and the study of public administration, in that it seeks to find out in what ways institutional design affects communication flows between citizens and government, so that citizens cooperate with each other more effectively and achieve collective action, that is so they see it as in their interests to contribute to public goods (Ostrom 1990).

Public goods are the positive externalities associated with pro-social behaviour change, that is benefits that have collective advantage, but which are not in the short-term interests of people to contribute to, partly because they fear bearing the cost, or they think there is no point doing small actions that are unlikely on their own to make a difference. Policies designed with behavioural insights might be seen to cumulate to facilitate collective action, and to promote greater trust in others and in government. Such policies may convey signals that ask people to contribute to public goods, either based on people's understanding the wider social purpose or with the policies operating subliminally without recipients being aware of the social benefits. In this way, behavioural public policies operate within the moral economy of private actions, whereby people can be encouraged to act in ways that are pro-social and overcome their sense of self-interest (Bowles 2016). Individuals are not entirely the rational non-co-operators described in basic game theory, such as the players in a prisoner's dilemma. But there still remains the problem of conveying an effective signal in a way that generates collective action, and encourages individuals to perceive societal and their own incentives as working together, which is not easy to achieve.

THE TOOLS OF GOVERNMENT

Nudge can address more fundamental aspects of behaviour by working with the existing tools of government. By reforming how the tools of government work, such as with taxes or regulations, behavioural public policy can improve their traction so that citizens willingly change their behaviour for the public good. In that sense, the ambit of behavioural public policy is much wider than the nudge stereotype indicates and includes applying behavioural insights to all actions of government rather than just to information flows between citizens and the state. For example, a tax change, which appears to be as far from a nudge as can be imagined, can change behaviour with no reference to behavioural insights, but it will be all the more effective if designed with them in mind (e.g. Chetty et al. 2009; Chetty and Saez 2013). Legal reforms need to be introduced with awareness of the informational environment if they are to be effective, even if the use of the behavioural sciences involves some careful thinking about the purpose of law and its relation to democratic processes (Alemanno and Sibony 2015). In these ways, the conventional tools of government can be refashioned using the ideas of behavioural science. The claim is that all tools of government are informational at root and current research can refine and improve their effectiveness (John 2013a).

The wider applicability of nudge to the tools of government has prompted some to recommend that government should use behavioural science to force citizens to move away from their existing behaviours rather than nudge them (Marteau et al. 2011). Behavioural ideas can more effectively compel people to change their behaviours than nudge, which is seen to be more of an encomium. It involves using the power of the state to sanction changes when they are needed rather than rely on situations where citizens can opt out or refuse if they want. In spite of wanting to go beyond the more limited range of messaging policies, compulsion is not the approach of this book. It would be counter-productive to develop a super-science of public administration so the tools of government become directive in character, even though some of these efforts can be useful in the right context. In the end, top-down behavioural policies, even when refined by testing, will fail because of the entrenched ideas and embedded behaviours of citizens. The result may be some short-term changes in behaviour, but not the uplift that policy-makers and voters are looking for. Citizens increasingly resist such commands and find ways to avoid regulations, which is the result of the loss of authority of government and other expert voices, and the spread of democratic ideas of self-ownership. Command and control often just do not work on their own as strategies. It is better to work within sets of human expectations and relationships, along the grain of habits and values of both policy-makers and citizens, so that both connect to each other in better ways, which involves respecting the autonomy of each in the process. In that sense, no one wants nudge policies to be effective in getting the police to arrest suspects more quickly, or in inculcating fear among taxpayers; instead, the nudges of Thaler and Sunstein appeal more to people's good nature to get them to pay taxes on time or report crimes and so on. It can be finely balanced between using nudges to get better tool design and using psychological insights for commands and controls. A middle approach is advocated by Oliver (2013b), who argues for *budges*, which indicate a wider range of policy options than nudges. Overall, the desired balance of behavioural insights is to have as many responsive nudges as possible and choose ones that build on democratically agreed policies and procedures rather than rely on top-down controls. With these considerations in mind, policy-makers are in a good position to seize the opportunity to develop more decentralised and reflective nudges.

This focus on certain kinds of intervention has the advantage of not extending the definition of nudge to every action of government that uses a psychological insight in some way, which could be construed to be anything that government does. It avoids concept stretching, which Sartori (1970) complained about in studies in political science. Nudges remain as light-touch human-centric policies and prompts. But opportunities to find them exist right across the spectrum of public activities.

NUDGE AND THE IMPLEMENTATION OF PUBLIC POLICIES

As well as operating across the range of tools and instruments, nudging can operate within the implementation chain of policies. A successful policy relies on a chain of interactions within bureaucracies as well as feedback and interdependence between citizens and public organisations. A behavioural approach can examine each link in the chain, find out about the behavioural cues needed to improve the transmission of commands and responsiveness to context, and then improve the delivery of the policy. It is hard for a behavioural intervention on one element of the implementation process to work if other parts of the delivery chain are not fully functioning. Reforming more than one link in the chain, making the improvements in delivery, can fan into the whole administrative process. Positive feedback can improve the working of all the sequences in the implementation process and generate better policy outcomes, as all actors benefit from the resulting synergy. This strategy also requires repeated interventions to tweak the implementation process.

This opportunity for using behavioural public policy addresses concerns long expressed by theorists of implementation about the likelihood of policy failure and the importance of improving the causal links in the implementation process by better theories about what works (Pressman and Wildavsky 1973). A key challenge is how a sponsor agency can ensure a delivery agency implements a policy faithfully. Behavioural insights inform work on implementation by moving beyond seeing policy outputs just as a summation of desired changes. Instead, as implied, for example, by cybernetic approaches to implementation (Dunsire 1993), improvement happens more effectively because of system-wide communications and positive feedback, which do not need to be guided step-by-step. Other recent studies of implementation have focused on learning, stimulated by better leadership and close attention to detail (Coelho and Ratnoo 2015). Behavioural insights can be the route to forging these better links, by careful appraisal of the causal steps and encouraging positive feedback up and down the delivery chain.

ENTREPRENEURIAL PUBLIC ADMINISTRATION

Behavioural public policy is usually practised by bureaucrats who are located in agencies. They have power and legitimacy to act from the authorisation of politicians. In such a context, doing behavioural policy might seem to be straightforward. It requires decision-makers to embrace the ideas of behavioural science and improve their evidence collection procedures. They then can put into place interventions that make best use of these ideas: hence nudge units and behavioural policy initiatives tested with randomised controlled trials (or other forms of rigorous evaluation) as discussed above. Such a move can help reinvigorate bureaucracies by making them more evidence based, more imaginative in their thinking, and increasingly willing to challenge existing ideas and standard operating procedures. Behavioural public policy can give power to the experts and those with track records of innovation, which can then spread across agencies in a pattern of diffusion. In this way, a more entrepreneurial public administration might come about (John 2014). This expansion of interest can widen the purview of behaviour change policies; the diffusion of new practices might help bureaucrats develop policies without the frequent need for experts or nudge units; and it might lead to a try-and-test approach to developing and introducing policies.

Experimental or entrepreneurial public administration does of course have to be matched against all the forces in bureaucracies that keep them operating in path-dependent ways. They adapt in response to new ideas, but they are probably more interested in long-term survival by effectively gaming the adoption of new practices. As a result of this strategic behaviour, organisations survive, ready for the next set of new ideas promoted by think tanks and academic champions. In fact, to ensure longevity, the successful adoption of nudge requires skilful advocacy on the part of intellectuals and bureaucrats, who are sensitive to the needs of agencies, keen to deliver improvements to services and to save money, careful not to risk politically sensitive interventions, and are responsive to the pragmatic instincts of heads of large departments and delivery units (John 2017b).

With the success of nudge units in assisting government policy, it may be the case that the very adaptability of behavioural insights reveals nudge to be a conservative phenomenon, or more conservative than it should be, largely because of its ability to be easily translated, that is to be in tune with the preferences of administrators and politicians, whose interests might limit the potential range of nudge and disguise its potential radicalism. Such a concern about the underlying agenda of behavioural change and its potential range is the reason for the question in this book's title: How far to nudge? Nudgers have taken pragmatic and understandable routes to promote the successful use of behavioural insights; the question is whether there is a potential for a wider and deeper use of behavioural ideas so increasing the scope of nudge. In an initial answer to how far to nudge, this book's argument suggests that reformers and academics could apply behavioural insights much more extensively than they do now. The early innovations in behavioural public policies are just the beginning rather than an end point for the research and policy programme. It is a good time to bank the gains and move on.

THE PROMISE OF THINK: NUDGE PLUS

The secret of more radical nudges is to consider public policy in terms of how citizens perceive their own actions and those of public officials, especially as they unfold over the long term. Policy-makers need to respond to citizens and act consistently with their preferences. To an extent, citizens need to be involved in and debate the policy changes that might be directed to their own behaviours. This is the agenda of think, which can be seen as an alternative to nudge (John et al. 2011), and is close to ideas argued for by those who believe in deliberative public policy. Debate, self-ownership, and collective decision-making are the key ways of achieving behaviour change. People are given information to debate the issues; they have the space to deliberate; and then policies may be changed as a result for collective benefit (Fung 2006). A range of democratic innovations across the world can harness this willingness of people to get involved in different ways (Smith 2009). The main problem with think is that it is hard to get these initiatives off the ground, ensure policy-makers use these procedures, and implement the recommendations of deliberative exercises. People self-select into these activities, making for an unrepresentative sample of the population involved, and nowhere near large enough to scale up to generate the shift in policy outcomes needed for mass behaviour change. Citizen participation exercises on their own often are characterised by low participation and minority representation. Such is also the fate of citizen juries and other deliberative forums. These interventions can also be expensive to implement. They seem to be better when addressing thorny public problems, such as the siting of a nuclear power plant, rather than the day-to-day issues of behaviour change, such as weight loss. In contrast, nudge initiatives are easy to implement, cheap to do, get the buy-in of policy-makers, do not need much effort or even conscious awareness on the part of citizens, and have an immediate impact on behaviours and in due course policy outcomes.

But nudge is closer to think than might be imagined, especially in how it works in practice. The claim of this book is that nudging is much more than giving messages or creating defaults; it requires some thought on the part of citizens to respond to signals from public organisations and their political principals. In other words, for nudge to work in better ways there should be a consideration about how citizens understand the wider choices in public policy implied by nudges. Citizens may need to understand the wider policy issues so as to be influenced by behavioural cues. Consider, for example, a nudge seeking to get people to turn up to a doctor's appointment on time (Hallsworth et al. 2015), which points out the costs to the publicly-funded health service of missed appointments. In one sense, the nudge could be seen as just a prompt, activating a subliminal belief that turning up on time is a good idea, and it is just the busyness of everyday life that has caused the patient not to arrive on time. But, in another, this nudge relies on the respondent understanding that resources are tight, that it is bad to waste resources and that turning up on time has an effect on the quality of the service overall, and having a belief that the money saved will be beneficial. In other words, the nudge depends on people having thought about the complex public policy issues, which is the reason that behavioural cues and prompts are being considered by decision-makers. They need to know that it is a public policy problem. It is more than just being reminded of their civic obligations. Then also a degree of trust is needed on the part of citizens. Citizens need to know that people in charge of the system overall are striving to make it work better.

It is important for people to rein in their short-term desires and to act collectively. It also implies that citizens are not acting from short-term self-interest, where it may make sense not to turn up because of other things happening that are more pressing, where citizens think that the doctor will be free at another time and the appointment can be rearranged. A message asking someone to turn up on time implies that citizens think about their duties and obligations. It implies they know what it means to be an effective citizen. The same is true of asking people to pay their taxes on time. If taxpayers only thought about it selfishly they would weigh up the costs of non-compliance against the benefit in paying late, which yields the prediction that the nudge would not work, because it is hard for the exchequer to chase up everyone effectively, or people may behave strategically by paying at the last minute or incurring the cost of a penalty that is small compared to the benefits on cash flow and interest payments of not paying early. The nudge works better if it is part of a long-term conversation between the state and citizens about what is the role of citizens in public services, and about the relationship between individuals and the state. This kind of thinking might not need to be explicit, but it is implied in the ways in which nudges actually work in practice, even if citizens are not always thinking about the reasons and assumptions that are being conveyed.

The challenge for policy-makers is to ensure that some degree of reflection or thinking is integrated into the design and delivery of behavioural interventions so as to encourage citizen responsiveness. The opportunity for nudge is to deliver interventions in such a way that citizens can be involved and reflect upon their actions, an inclusive form of nudge that is transparent with the public. There is a wider debate about the use of ideas about behaviour change, but without the assumptions about citizen capacity made by deliberative democrats.

There is then a radical agenda at the heart of behaviour change policies, which can address core questions of political organisation and even representation, as it is based on re-establishing good relationships between citizens and governments. It is only when the citizens are involved with the decisions that affect them that long-term solutions to public policy problems are possible. In this way, citizens can automate the changes brought about by nudge and integrate them into their routines and habits. They are nudged to think and then they habituate the acquired behaviours. This claim is at the heart of crafting behavioural public policy, that is policy founded on understanding the behaviours of citizens, but also embraces their capacity to reflect and participate in joint ventures by taking them seriously.

Such actions may be prompted by the nudge directly, but nudge can aim to get citizens to address the issue themselves with a little help. Citizens might lack the capacity to think through the issues or have the right level of information to make an informed choice. Nudges become what Hertwig (2017) calls boosts (see also Grüne-Yanoff and Hertwig 2016). Hertwig writes that 'boosts explicitly seek to foster existing decision-making competences and to develop new ones, thus enabling individuals to translate their intentions (preferences) into behaviour – that is, to exercise personal agency'. The effect is indirect, but moves away from the technocratic approach so common with nudges. Boosts are a bit like the thinks that John et al. (2011) tested, but are closer to nudges and more deliverable. In Hertwig's (2017) argument, people sometimes need help in understanding complex choices, such as which medical procedure to choose, which they are increasingly asked to do in an age of consumer choice and sovereignty. They may not understand the statistics of probability, but a few tips and guides might help them make better decisions. These interventions are sometimes called 'educative nudges', which are about transmitting skills and ideas, rather than automating desired behaviours.

In the argument of John and Stoker (2017), these kinds of strategies build on the original nudges, but they take them further, perhaps not as far as think, but a little way toward that goal consistent with what social scientists know about people's limited capacity for reflection, constraints on time, and their need for immediate effects, even if the approach is also about building a long-term partnership between citizens and the state. They call this approach 'nudge plus', which is to emphasise how nudges can be broadened outwards, so as to incorporate boosts and citizen thoughts about public policies. This stimulation of thinking is desirable so as to move beyond the more technocratic considerations of the nudge agenda as currently practised. Nudge plus amplifies nudges and makes them more democratic.

There is a greater interest in the behavioural sciences in securing long-term change rather than the short-lived uplifts that characterise the classic early nudge interventions, such as tax changes and prompts to encourage charitable giving. Scientists and policy-makers know that the effects of interventions can last a long time, but these are usually maintained because of habit or discovering a new form of behaviour, which might be unconscious. There is now much more of an interest in developing self-sustaining behaviours that might operate across a range of activities that complement each other, so that people do more exercise, eat better, drink less, and so on, and this might translate into other behaviours and activities, so citizens get a new perspective on their lives as a result of reading across a range of their behaviours and seeing the links between them. This is what psychologists call a 'passion for long-term goals', or 'grit' (Duckworth et al. 2007). This commitment is not related to IQ, and moderately to education: the implication is that individuals can cultivate grit, in a long-term programme of behaviour change. Some of the nudges that are seeking to change people's goals, such as commitment devices that are keeping people on track, are about trying to get individuals on a path of change, and this requires people to consider their situations and then put into place measures that will change their behaviours, even if every step on the subsequent pathway is not consciously reflected upon.

So far, the kinds of nudges described earlier in this chapter have not fully addressed either thinks or the sustaining of interventions, partly because of the pragmatic agenda followed by nudge units and other advocates, designed to encourage agencies to use behavioural science and to bed down behavioural insights into the normal business of making and implementing policies. Given the success of nudge, now is the time to broaden it out and to link it more closely to democratic practice.

SYSTEM-WIDE CHANGES

The aim with nudge, boost, or nudge plus is not to use a behavioural insight to create a one-off change, but to promote a state or environment where these interventions help establish a new equilibrium of self-reinforcing and beneficial behaviours, whereby all benefit, and there is not a huge daily effort to keep the new behaviours in place. The end result is something like the *Highway Code*, which in the UK is a set of codified rules that are not legally enforceable and that govern how people drive their cars. They assist good driving to the benefit of all, but nobody enforces this; it is a self-regulating system of rules. The behaviours follow from a common understanding and internalised norms. People don't need to think about the code and may have forgotten it long after passing their driving test, having mugged up on it in order to get through. But it still influences their behaviour and on reflection most people consider it a good thing to follow. Of course, a highway code is not a perfect system of nudging. People do not always obey it, especially in metropolitan centres like London. A pedestrian might find it hard to rely on cars following the code, for example acting on road signs. Many motorists might behave selfishly and only follow the code strategically to avoid hitting other cars. But such imperfections are bound to be the case in any informal scheme, which is why there is a need for policy-makers to try to shape these understandings by nudges. The key question is how to get to a more self-sustaining implementation system and whether some reflection as well as nudging is needed to improve such codes and introduce them for every kind of behaviour. The nudge creates the reflection that causes people to adopt the code; then automatic and self-monitoring processes sustain the behaviours over time, as well as daily interactions with others who also observe the practice. The code creates a set of norms that are maintained over time by habit and fear of not abiding by them. The nudge becomes the initial shift that sets off an upward cycle of desired behaviours, one action that is part of a system of reinforcing actions, with occasional repeated nudges to keep everyone on track.

In fact, behavioural interventions need to be seen as part of a complex system with moving parts (Spotswood 2016). The designer needs to think about how to move from one equilibrium point to another, an insight which reflects recent progress in the economic analysis of experiments (Banerjee and Duflo 2014). The interest in using experiments is not just to show that there is a one-off change, which might in fact put a system out of equilibrium; rather they should show how the balance of interests and interactions can shift to a new pattern of cooperation and regulation that is both beneficial and self-sustaining.

Another example is smoking bans, such as the one introduced in England that prohibited cigarette and other smoking in workplaces, particularly in bars, cafes, and clubs where staff work but where people used to like to smoke. These laws have the appearance of central government compelling people not to smoke indoors. In reality, the laws follow public opinion and considerable debate about what needs to happen. There need to be considerable changes to the political and policy agenda beforehand. Once the ground has been laid for a reform, the legislation can create a new equilibrium point, which ends up with people willingly not smoking in public places. Smokers internalise the norm of not smoking inside, agreeing with the principle behind the legislation. They nudge each other. Light-touch reminders from public authorities are all that is needed to sustain the practice over time. No enforcement needs to occur, as those who smoke consent to the rules, which on the whole they believe to be fair. They do not even need to think about obeying the rules, which they come to do automatically. The question becomes what interventions might start off the process of accepting regulatory changes and the establishment of a stable system of self-reinforcing behaviours, and whether people can be nudged in ways that support a system change.

This attention to the underlying support for institutional and behavioural outcomes is a more radical version of nudge and takes the agenda to a wide-ranging set of actions and behaviours. The agenda of this book is to radicalise nudge and to extend its insights, as a way of answering the question in the book's title. With talk of the system of interactions, it becomes vital to include the policy-makers as part of the conversation, and these people should be expected to change their behaviours too, which provides a further extension of nudge, as the next section elaborates.

TURNING THE TABLES ON THE POLICY-MAKERS

There is a paradox: the use of behavioural policies requires the upholding of the ideal of the classic rational politician or bureaucrat who carefully weighs up the evidence and then follows the best course of action. But this is just what behavioural science says does not occur: decision-makers should be just as responsive to cues and limited in their capacity to weigh evidence as the citizens they hope to influence. This bias occurs in spite of official support and the backing of experts who advise policy-makers. Often heuristics take precedence because of the speed of decision-making. Decision-makers prefer to rely on their own instincts and act out of habit (Loewen et al. 2014; Lodge and Wegrich 2016). This argument appeared in the classic works of public administration, as set out by its founding scholars in the 1950s, in particular by Simon (1947, 1955), who formulated the concept of bounded rationality. These ideas reappeared in Allison's famous book *Essence of Decision* (1971). Such concepts are consistent with formal models of politics that emphasise search costs.

The limited cognitive range of politicians and bureaucrats may mean that nudge becomes the preserve of the enthusiast or the follower of fashion. Politicians are locked into existing routines and sources of information, with new ways of working involving risks and potentially negative outcomes. Indeed, prospect theory says they would avoid making decisions that have potentially negative or perceived negative outcomes. In practice, some politicians take risks and are not fully aware of the negative outcomes. Rather than considering the costs of system redesign and being aware of the risks of adopting new policies (testing them through trials), they are more interested in being able to claim credit for acting in the short term. The bureaucrats who adopt behavioural insights may be those who benefit from being innovative or being different from the mainstream, or risk-takers. There is the danger that the behavioural interventions will be the wrong ones, and done from advocacy, fashion, and the norms of behavioural science. It is a case of the blind leading the blind.

In the end the limited human cognitions of elected politicians and bureaucrats offer an opportunity for citizens and citizen groups to use the self-same techniques of behavioural science to influence politicians in ways that are more direct than elections and public deliberation. The spread of the use of behavioural ideas beyond government gives an opportunity for citizens to turn the tables on their governors. They can nudge politicians and bureaucrats. In this way, there is an opportunity to move away from the paternalistic and technocratic assumptions of the existing version of behavioural policy and to open up government using a variety of nudges and cues, which might be an achievable conversation to have, and one that might be feasible given the resistance by citizens to deliberative exercises that need high levels of time and commitment. The result is that politicians, bureaucrats, and citizens are engaged in a shared project, both to use behavioural techniques and to work out what they are for. All can learn as part of this process, which involves interaction. Citizens are happier to influence politicians who have more limited formal rationality. All are human and need external stimuli to get to the best course of action.

CONCLUSION

In this book, the meaning and scope of behavioural public policy are set out. It is seen as an ideal to which bureaucrats, citizens, and politicians can aspire. The claim is that thinking in terms of behavioural solutions can help policy-makers address public problems, but that part of the solution is the engagement of citizens in problem-solving activities. The result is bureaucracies that are not only adept in using behavioural ideas and testing them experimentally, but also are responsive. The solution to current policy problems is about joint problem-solving between citizens and bureaucrats, where each recognises the limits of the other in terms of time and capacity in making decisions.

This book goes beyond many publications in the field of nudge, while paying due homage to the important books and papers that have come before. It seeks to apply the perspective of a political scientist and public administration scholar: that is, to see the application of behavioural policy as a feature of politics that needs to be viewed as a consequence of conscious decisions to implement and to introduce behavioural policies, and that has to be argued for within bureaucracies and implemented using standard frameworks for delivery. The book aims to understand the impact of behavioural policies within bureaucracies and how they operate. It seeks to set out the wider context of nudge in terms of citizen responsiveness to the measures proposed, which implies some degree of conscious consent about the proposals and an element of debate, even if done internally in people's minds as they make decisions. The book sets out the ideal of a more behavioural policy system, where policy-makers consider the interests of citizens when they formulate public policies and where citizens reflect upon and automate the behavioural cues that are produced by decision-makers. Citizens become part of the solution by using the behavioural sciences to get responses from policy-makers, and policy-makers stimulate other policy-makers in searching for a responsive and experimental public administration. The aim is to create a system of behaviours that positively reinforce each other.

There is a massive opportunity to be grasped. Too often large policy programmes fail because they do not address the behavioural determinants of policy outcomes; in particular, policy-makers often do not understand the very human reasons why measures and interventions fail. It is possible to use an understanding of human behaviour to solve these problems and change policy outcomes for billions of people across the world. It is desirable to use theories of behaviour change to improve the capacity of the government so it works much better than it does currently. Given the desirability of the basic objectives, the question is how far should policy-makers and reformers go? Can they go much further than they do currently? This book asks these questions and aims to provide answers, with the implication that reformers and policy-makers can nudge more than they do currently, and governments, when they are formulating and implementing nudge policies, can act in ways that are consistent with liberal ideals and uphold a responsive and rights-respecting system of public authority that citizens in a democracy rightly expect. By keeping a bottom-up perspective, working from the perspective of citizens and treating decision-makers as human actors, the potential of nudge can be seized in ways that enhance democratic ideals and are consistent with ethical goals.

PLAN OF THE BOOK

The approach of the book is bottom up: to explore the public problems that give rise to the challenges and then to see how writers and thinkers stumbled on the solutions. The starting place, in Chapter 2, is the nature of the problems that governments face. This chapter sets out the key policy problems facing government and why they are sustained by entrenched behaviours. It contains a more detailed review of some policy problems, such as obesity. It assesses why conventional policy instruments often fail.

Once the problems have been reviewed, the intellectual history starts in Chapter 3, as knowledge from the academy is very important in explaining what happened later on when policies were being formulated. The chapter reviews the extensive literature on behaviour change, and in particular is interested in the debates that occurred in the 1960s and 1970s that emerged from the research of Kahneman and Tversky. Even though the concepts of bias and judgement are not entirely original to these authors, the pair developed these ideas into a research programme that had a profound influence on economics and on social science thinking in general. Even though there have been debates in sub-disciplines, such as the psychology of health or social marketing, they have not had the profound influence of the founders of behavioural economics. Readers may be familiar with the review of behavioural policy problems in Chapter 2, and they may know the story of behavioural economics and other related studies in Chapter 3. If so, they may skip or briefly skim these chapters without risking not understanding the key arguments and claims that come later on.

The modern story starts in Chapter 4. The chapter is about the way in which ideas in the academy got into the mainstream, through the natural processes of influence and the role of advocates and entrepreneurs. There is an account of how nudge has been enhanced by its popularisation and has come to be seen to be common sense in its application, but also limited in its radicalism in that certain routes have been taken but not others. This argument, which is about path dependence, continues in Chapter 5, which considers how nudge has been used by policy-makers, which been propagated by nudge units and other agencies keen on applying behavioural insights. The chapter contains a review of the classic nudges, such as on letter redesigns and organ donation. This chapter also tells the reader about the policy innovations brought about by research in the behavioural sciences, but with an eye to what choices have been made and whether other opportunities could have been seized.

Chapter 6 starts to build up the core argument of the book by looking at some common criticisms of nudge, particularly over its range and the power of its findings. Even though many of these criticisms of nudge are overdone, the process of explaining them prompts the thought about what kinds of intervention could be stronger and more self-sustaining. Chapter 7 is about the ethical dimension to behavioural interventions, which again has attracted a lot of critical opinion, in particular about the consistency of the arguments Thaler and Sunstein have put forward, and the sense of unease people have felt about the way in which nudge appears to be manipulative and to reduce people's autonomy. Thinking about this problem leads to the argument for a more agent-centred version of nudge, which is the basis of the radical version argued for in this book. Chapter 8, called 'Nudge plus and how to get there', is a presentation of the central proposals of the book, which are about the potential for a more open, reflective, and decentralised form of nudging, with examples and a discussion of the potential for their use. Chapter 8 also contains a discussion of elite nudges and how these may be extended to a wider range of phenomena as part of bottom-up nudging. Chapter 9 is intended to pull the book together to answer the question 'How far to nudge?', taking into account practical limitations and the salience of politics. It comes to an overall assessment about the future potential of behavioural public policy.

2. Behavioural public problems

This chapter is devoted to explaining why human behaviour is so important for achieving desired public policy outcomes. It is important to establish this claim, so it becomes more than a truism. The truism would take the following form: because all public policies are implemented through changes or assumptions about human behaviour, behaviour is important in public policy. But this statement can be seen to be tautological in that any form of human behaviour has to be considered part of public policy, as most policies involve humans as subjects in their design and implementation. The behavioural argument has to be much stronger. It should take the causal form that certain behavioural traits and biases detrimentally affect policy outcomes in ways that are systematic, knowable, and fixable. The whole point of behavioural public policy is to correct for certain kinds of behaviour, in particular those traits that reinforce poor policy outcomes. People do not make good choices for themselves, which is the justification for the nudges of the Thaler and Sunstein sort, which can be seen in many fields, such as health, saving for retirement, and seeking better attainment in education.

One important point to take account of when considering behavioural causes of public problems is that the nature of the behaviour varies according to the outcome, which means that there are different behavioural problems at play and varied solutions that may be adopted. With some problems, it is question of individual choices, which are not greatly dependent on each other, even though they may have an impact on the costs of public services, such as in health. Other behavioural problems require citizens to cooperate with each other and have a reasonable expectation that others are going to act as well or else their own contribution would be too small to make any difference and they would bear all the costs. This feature of some social relationships is what social scientists call the 'collective action problem' – the idea that people might want to change their behaviour but because they are uncertain about the choices of others they go for a safe strategy, which often means not cooperating or doing anything (see Ostrom 1990). Some kinds of behaviours, such as pro-environmental behaviours, suffer from this problem and thus require different kinds of intervention from government or other agencies in response. The implication is that the tools of behaviour change need to be adapted to deal with the nature of the problems being addressed.

These behavioural factors need to be considered alongside other causes of policy problems, whether they have their origins in technological or scientific changes, economic and social factors or even the actions of policy-makers themselves, which often reinforce behavioural public problems. Different sectors of activity vary in the extent to which individual behaviour is the cause. A judgement needs to be made about the balance and nature of the interrelationships, and where individual action depends on other policy levers being in place, rather than individuals having to bear the burden of achieving behaviour changes and delivering favourable policy outcomes on their own even if nudged by government. The tendency to assume that individual behaviour is the sole source of a public problem needs to be avoided when formulating behavioural public policy.

To begin, this chapter explores the sources of behavioural problems by examining the case of health, which provides a relatively straightforward example of behavioural problems, before looking at more complex examples, such as the environment.

THE NATURE OF THE PROBLEM: AN EXAMPLE FROM FOOD AND DIET

Consider a basic activity such as the consumption of food. In past generations, people had limited supplies, in particular of protein, and had to make do with a mixed diet of some meat, but mainly vegetables and fruits. This diet was particularly observed in countries bordering the Mediterranean, where there were few sources of meat but a lot of natural produce, such as olive oil, and where vegetables were easy to grow. But it also was followed in countries in the north of Europe, where meat was only a bit more plentiful, at least for the large majority of the population. Most people were engaged in manual work. While these populations could be hit by disease and while even minor cuts and wounds could not be effectively treated before the arrival of penicillin, most people were healthy and not overweight, because they had to exercise and the foods available happened to be healthy. Move forward a couple of hundred years to the 2010s, especially in the urban centres, and this diet has largely vanished as the norm, with people consuming more meat, which is high in fat. Fewer fresh vegetables are eaten. New products that are cheap to buy and convenient to eat contain a lot of sugar, fat and salt, all of which are bad for health. People do not exercise very much, as they drive cars or can move about without physical effort on public transport. Many people have become sedentary. Some are overweight or obese. They are likely to get strokes, heart attacks, and cancer as they get older, in spite of advances in life expectancy from better health care, rising incomes and changing occupations. In some ways, it was not the fault of the individuals that the healthier (if riskier) environment that imposed exercise and a better diet went away. Growing prosperity and technology are to blame. Human beings like to eat until they are full, often eating what is on the plate or just the available food to hand. People would rather sit on the sofa than exercise. Sweet foods are generally nicer – evolution told people to like them as sources of energy when food supplies were meagre. Watching television or playing computer games is much more fun than running on a machine in the gym. But the result is that the behaviours that come naturally are very harmful and impose high costs for the individual and for society too in terms of health care costs and reduced labour productivity. An obesity epidemic is in train (Branca et al. 2007). Individual human behaviour is the main cause, which is influenced by the availability of foods, the activities of private companies, the role of the media and advertising, and even government policy.

BENEFICIAL BEHAVIOURS IN HEALTH

A change in eating habits and some modest exercise, such as walking, can have large effects. To achieve these changes, governments have tried to educate through public service adverts and advice by doctors. Healthy lifestyles have been promoted by journalists and television programme makers. The middle classes have become aware of these advantages, so healthy eating and exercise have become fashionable without much prompting by government. The hope is that these behaviours can diffuse more generally across society, but in practice a lot of people do not want to act on the information or wish to be influenced by the middle classes. Alternatively, they may accept the argument and understand what the science is saying, but not be motivated enough to change their behaviour.

Governments can try to get people to change their behaviour through education and encouragement, but it is hard to shift behaviours. Consider the need for regular exercise to probe this argument further. Exercise is a classic form of behaviour that has strong beneficial effects. Research on 1 million adults found that exercise of about one hour a day can help them avoid premature death, making a 60 per cent difference in outcomes

(Ekelund et al. 2016). The researchers did a systematic review of six databases to locate cohort studies (the same people observed over time), which had information on daily sitting, television-viewing time and physical activity, to look for the impact on mortality, heart disease, and forms of cancer, and were able to account for other causes of ill health, such as obesity and smoking. The clear finding is that lack of exercise causes negative health outcomes. What is interesting from this study is that it found that just one hour of exercise reduces the negative health effect of sedentary behaviour, even of television-watching, though this is still harmful. But it is important to be careful in forming conclusions from a longitudinal study in which exercise co-varies with health, as confounding factors that might cause people both to be sedentary and to have ill health are not fully considered. This argument is stronger for the television link, as people might retreat indoors if they have less inclination to go outside because they are isolated and depressed, which causes them to become unhealthy. Yet overall it is true that lack of exercise is correlated strongly with poor health outcomes. The scale of the problem is massive, with only 25 per cent of adults in the US doing the very minimum amount of exercise of half an hour a day five days a week (U.S. Department of Health and Human Services 2010).

RESISTANCE TO BEHAVING WELL

Small changes in behaviour can change outcomes quite strongly. But why do people keep behaving in harmful ways? One cause is a lack of options: at work the job task and the design of the office make sitting almost inevitable. There may be long tasks to complete, such as serving customers or completing routines on the computer. People might not take breaks, wanting to keep in front of their screens to check e-mails. There may be nobody else who goes out of the office at lunchtime to encourage others. It may be a noisy polluted street, so people feel it is not worth going out, let alone exercising. Even motivated individuals might not want to do some exercise during break times. In this way, change in the external world (e.g. changes in work patterns) links to other incentives and social norms that can embed low exercise as a repeated activity.

Behaviour comes about from mental processes, in which behavioural intentions are important. Such intentions come from an underlying set of attitudes based on beliefs and people's evaluation of likely outcomes. Affecting behaviour is people's subjective norm, linked to their normative beliefs and motivation to comply; important too is their perceived sense of control, which is affected by their efficacy, or the belief that they can change matters for themselves. This is the theory of planned behaviour (Fishbein and Ajzen 1975; Ajzen 1985). People may have intentions to change their behaviour but in fact do not, so that the status quo and the behaviours that sustain weak outcomes are maintained over time. Norms and the social environment in which people live have an influence in limiting the willingness to engage in behaviours that may improve outcomes. People may want to engage in a particular behaviour, but social factors and norms may prevent it from happening.

Behaviours shaped by peers and families are often enjoyable, even addictive, so hard to change once adopted. The effects of these behaviours are delayed for many decades, so people cannot see the long-term consequences of their actions, and may think that nothing will happen to them. Because not everyone develops negative health outcomes – at first at least – people might think themselves immune or lucky, which the lack of immediate consequences might encourage them to think. Their calculation of risk is very poor, but hard to correct. Bald statistics are often meaningless to many people who do not understand them. Such statistics can be countered by a sense of being lucky, a feeling that you deserve one luxury and a belief that you are cutting down (no matter how unjustified this is). People deceive themselves and rationalise their behaviours, screening out messages they do not like to hear. The question becomes what measures and actions can be taken by government to break through such arguments that people make to themselves.

Health is a field where there are clearly identifiable behaviours individuals can change to make their own outcomes a lot better but that also have large collective benefits in terms of the saving of public resources, which can be reinvested in other areas where behaviour is less of a cause and there are therefore other forms of treatment. Lung cancer, for instance, is mainly caused by smoking tobacco. A behaviour change involving giving up smoking tobacco will lead to large reductions in health expenditure from treating cancer and other diseases caused by smoking, such as emphysema and hardening of the arteries, but in addition to the benefits to society the individual will still be massively better off. A lower consumption of alcohol can also lead to reduced public expenditure (or reduced insurance contributions for all), for example on treatment for cirrhosis and other health disorders.

HABITS

The other dimension to the resistance of people to messages is the prevalence of unconscious processes that cause them to continue the harmful behaviours. People automate the behaviours into their routines, so they become habitual, adopted because people have behaved similarly in the past, which makes their repetition reassuring. Over time habits may strengthen (Denford et al. 2016: 56). Habits once set are hard to break. Even after behaviour change, old habits can reappear, with individuals trending back to their old behaviours. Habits can be useful in the other direction. Once a new behaviour has been stimulated, it can create a new habit, which beds down and is followed with just such a lack of reflection and self-awareness, with the difference being the benefit the individual gets from the action.

Behaviours are reinforced by the actions of outside bodies, which can use a variety of behavioural interventions to keep individuals consuming in the way they do, for organisational advantage. Private sector organisations spend a considerable amount of money on advertising to maintain expenditure on products that might not be healthy, especially smoking and alcohol, but also processed foods. Retailers engage in subtle interventions to change behaviours, such as in the design of supermarkets. As Marteau et al. (2011: 263) summarise,

> Shaping environments to cue certain behaviours is extremely effective, unfortunately often to the detriment of our health. The ready availability of foods that are packaged, presented, and engineered to stimulate our automatic, affective system has led us to consume more than is needed – consumption that is further primed by advertising. The doubling in alcohol consumption by young people over the past fifty years is attributed in part to its marketing and ready availability, and the design of many neighbourhoods supports car driving over walking or cycling.

Citizens are nudged then to act against their self-interest.

WHY CURRENT POLICIES DO NOT FULLY ADDRESS BEHAVIOUR CHANGE

In terms of thinking about how to deal with the problem of no exercise, governments seem to think that a large number of mainly educational initiatives, and demonstration projects to scale up initiatives, work well (see Reis et al. 2016), but very few are evaluated in a robust way, such as with randomised controlled trials. In fact, a behavioural perspective would be critical of such a blunderbuss approach that does not address the reasons why people do not behave as public professionals want them to. The public health approach would just see the lack of exercise as an information deficit needing encouragement and education. But if the endogeneity issue is seen as fundamental then there may be causes of the lack of willingness to exercise which are correlated with the outcome, such as mental health factors that impact on well-being and health and cause someone not to exercise. When considering many interventions around exercise, it is common to find that exercise is addressed at the same time as other behaviours, such as smoking, diet, and alcohol consumption (see Kahn et al. 2002: 76), making it hard to assess how the intervention actually addresses health outcomes.

Many information-based interventions have weak effects, for example the placing of signs next to lifts to encourage use of the stairs. Mass media campaigns also have moderate to no effects (Kahn et al. 2002: 78). Classroom interventions that have had a behavioural component (the learning of skills) have variable effects. Significant for this book, a more behavioural approach has better effects, such as systems of social support or the introduction of buddying. Effective too are environmental changes, such as changing the availability of exercise in terms of facilities. The conclusion to draw is that the information-informing approach is useful, but does not yield much, and a more behaviourally informed approach might work much better. It is possible to come to similar kinds of conclusions about other interventions designed to change people's behaviour, such as improved diet in low- and middle-income countries (World Health Organization 2009). Light interventions based on human agency do not appear to work, despite being favoured by many governments, such as the UK government's Change4Life programme, a campaign launched in 2009, aimed at children, to change eating habits (also see MangerBouger in France and Let's Move in the United States).

These campaigns appear to be tackling human behaviour, but they are essentially non-behavioural in that they are encouraging behaviour change; they do not use the full range of psychological traits, and perhaps focus on mechanisms that individuals do not find that easy to use: 'Exerting agency requires individuals to rally their cognitive, psychological, time, and material resources' (Adams et al. 2016). It requires too much of an individual's mental capacity to make sense of all that information and then act. It means that a lot of resources are expended on these campaigns, but they overload the individual and do not take advantage of more powerful mechanisms that require less effort.

The measures that appear to work for diet are targeted and directive (see Adams et al. 2016). The reason why such strong strategies can be the only ones that have a chance of working is the embedded nature of the behaviours that underpin the desired activities. It can be debated whether strong interventions, such as banning smoking in public places, are genuinely behavioural. The argument is that top-down interventions have to be behavioural or else they will not work. People can easily defy smoking bans; the only way to achieve compliance is by managing consent, which involves a lot of nudges before the activity is banned or restricted. These interventions then are closer to the nudge approach argued for in Chapter 1 where both information and institutional constraints are altered at the same time. In other words, is there a middle way between hard and soft interventions that economises on cognitive capacity but keeps individual freedom and agency?

RATIONAL ACTION AND BEHAVIOUR CHANGE

Often people do not act when it is clearly in their interests to do so. In economic theory behaviour should be the consequence of a balance of costs and benefits, so that actions that are harmful should be considered and then individuals do something about it. With some of the examples, such as health, it is possible to see clearly the advantage of a change in behaviour, so behaviour change is the logical consequence of a government providing more information. But, even with health, these kinds of campaigns are limited. Another way of looking at the problem is through an assessment of risk whereby individuals tend to overweight current benefits and down-weigh the costs. This can be rational in the sense that people might like smoking and drinking so much that they decide they would rather have the benefit now than later. The role of government is to inform people so they can find out whether they have exactly balanced out the costs and benefits. It is often the case that smokers know the costs of what they do but find it easy to down-weigh the actual costs or forget about them or justify the costs by statements along the lines of 'Smoking is my only pleasure.' This is at the heart of behaviour change interventions: whether the secret is to try to discover a rational core self that really wants to respond, which is the nudge approach, or whether the policy-maker just assumes irrationality and it is fine just to change the behaviour using this assumption. The key point is whether there are automatic processes that govern human behaviour that do not have their origins in cost–benefit thinking but derive from personal psychology. This means that human behaviour can be shaped by a set of external stimuli and prompts that are not about conveying the costs and benefits of decisions, but may relate to mood, emotions, intuitions, and senses of well-being in ways that are immediately responsive and not reflected upon. This may be a reaction against the perception of loss, and wanting to conform to the behaviour of other people.

There will be more on these points later in the book, but they show the importance of embeddedness and suggest that simple interventions based on altering the costs and benefits are usually limited in impact. That said, there is evidence that some cost–benefit interventions work, such as increases in the costs of alcohol per unit and paying for smoking cessation, which do not crowd out motivation.

REACTANCE

People often resist messages that come from an authority. This can be called 'reactance', which is a resistance to the activity when it appears that choices are being limited (Brehm 1966; Brehm and Brehm 1981). This phenomenon sounds surprising, because much of traditional public policy rests on the idea of experts finding out new pieces of information about what is beneficial or harmful for individuals. Governments then design policies to embody the information through advice, persuasion and regulation. Then citizens take note of the expert information, and adjust their behaviour accordingly. That model works where people trust those in authority and respect the role of experts; they put their faith in the politicians who make decisions for them. There is also a gradual diffusion of behaviours from early adopters to others, in processes of emulation that are based on respect and deference more generally. This model does not work in such a straightforward way today, partly because of the declining trust in experts and in government. Across a large number of indicators from surveys, standard messages of political trust show a decline, which is related to general social factors as well as to the performance of government (Dalton 2005). Dalton points out that the rates of decline are highest among the most highly educated groups in society. These are precisely the groups that are more receptive to messages about changing their behaviours, so this is damaging for the conventional tools of behaviour change. It is not just that citizens resist the idea of better behaviour change, but that the means of achieving it is different to a standard diffusion and deference model. Other steps are needed, ones that are attuned to the reference groups involved. For many interventions, there are different kinds of sub-groups that vary in their receptiveness to an intervention.

There are more precise reasons why a message to change behaviour might be resisted. People sometimes do not like to be told to do something. This can work in a simple way, with people resenting being told off, as a child does not like what might appear to be harsh words. People like approval and do not want disapproval, which might cause them to comply with a request, but it can cause them to resent it and maybe do the opposite to what is asked for. Sometimes the resistance can work in a subtle way. People comply with the request, but their secret self does not really want to do the activity: they might prefer to eat chocolates and sit in front of the television. Even though they comply with the intervention, after a while they return to the old activity, with the added enjoyment of it being a guilty pleasure; they might then do the condemned activity all the more because they like it, what is sometimes called a 'boomerang effect', similar to reactance. It can also be described as a 'backfire effect': when people receive corrective information their willingness to believe incorrect information increases (Nyhan and Reifler 2010). It appears to be linked to the strength with which the fact is associated with a person's identity. Reactance can happen when there is a lot of pressure to undertake the activity. Even strong eye contact with someone can provoke reactance (Chen et al. 2013). People do not like to be persuaded directly and will resist such messages, but this is what information campaigns often do.

MULTI-CAUSAL AND EMBEDDED BEHAVIOURS

In examining behaviours, it is tempting to focus on one kind and a single cause, and to see the solution as a focus on that behaviour, and then one lever or tool of government might solve the problem. Some of the health examples seem to point to this problem, so that smoking during pregnancy can be countered with a single intervention to change, such as an incentive. But in practice there are linked behaviours that lead to poor outcomes, which themselves have multiple causes, and which can then be reinforced over time by social norms and the influence of peers. A problem like alcoholism might be caused by personal factors, but in addition by the urban environment, low education, the influence of families, and cultural factors among social groups and their lifestyles (Annis et al. 1990: 17). The key idea is that these problems are embedded because behaviours are reinforced by the social environment and the influence of peer groups.

Behavioural problems are not just caused by individual psychology; they relate to how an individual is linked to other individuals and their social behaviours, which can often reinforce each other. Take the example of crime, which comes from people seeking a private benefit from illegal behaviours, or in acting out of impulse or anger in ways that harm people. There is a large literature about what causes crime, how it is embedded in social networks, and how people rarely make cost–benefit decisions about committing a crime. They may understate its costs and overestimate the benefits from the action, such as theft of property. It is the social networks that influence this kind of behaviour, and affect how information about criminal behaviour is transmitted. Once a person starts behaving in a criminal way, it is hard for that person to break out of the pattern, as a result of habit and the influence of peer groups. These behaviours may be reinforced by the criminal justice system and prison, which means that people's life chances are reduced and that they cannot get access to the job market, so making a life of crime apparently inevitable and making it likely that the pattern of recidivism will continue.

Problems themselves can be multiple and correlated with each other, so children who have behavioural problems in schools might also have problems at home; for example, through substance abuse they might develop psychological problems. As Gardner and Shaw (2008: 883) write on the problems of young children, 'Based on the relative instability of problem behavior during early childhood, it should not be surprising to learn that many children demonstrate multiple types of problem behavior, including co-occurring disruptive and emotional problems (e.g., oppositionality coupled with depression or attention deficit/hyperactivity disorder.' It follows that policies addressing such problems need to take account of these multiple causes.

In terms of societal problems, these examples may appear to be extreme, and also concentrated in sub-populations who are not numerous and already have a large amount of attention paid to them by public agencies with research programmes to back them up. But they form a subset of a large world of reinforced behaviours, which are just as likely to be the case in prosperous communities, but which have received less attention and are less visible. The point to make is that it can make it quite hard for an intervention to succeed, because of the force of these social factors driving behaviour and reinforcing each other. The nature of these behaviours can explain why informational or educational programmes often do not work, and it can then provide a justification for programmes of behaviour change. It can also give rise to pessimism as to whether these behaviours can be addressed in one-off interventions even of the nudge sort.

COLLECTIVE BEHAVIOURS

The attraction of the diet and exercise examples, and even crime, is that public interventions can be individually based without needing collective action on the part of the population. The intervention can be targeted to the individual and tailored accordingly. Even then, it is hard to shift behaviours, because they are tied up with people's lifestyles, structured by the work environment, supported by technology that everyone needs to use such as cars, and then influenced by peers. In the case of the environment, all these factors apply, but there is an additional problem that means that behaviours are even harder to shift. The issue is that individuals need to act jointly to ensure that environmental measures work. Consider a very simple environmental issue, such as littering. Here picking up an individual piece of litter does not make much of an impact on an urban street and also will not improve the welfare of the individual, who has to find a bin or pocket the piece of litter and take it home. Whereas the individual act of exercise has a direct beneficial impact for the individual (even feeling good after the exercise), the problem with not littering is that there is a cost, and the only reward is a feeling of having done some good. The problem is that interventions to improve the environment have to appeal to people's sense of the collective interest, but it is hard to appeal to these beliefs and values, making it difficult to shift behaviours in the long term. Also, if the intervention only shifts behaviour to a small degree, no one will notice the effect. Several fewer pieces of litter in the public park will hardly be spotted by anyone, which may de-incentivise the few people who responded to the anti-littering intervention. It is hard to question the claim that the behaviours will continue over time in the absence of strong enforcement. The book's discussion later on seeks to deal with the problem of inducing collective action without authoritarian and unfeasible interventions.

The same argument applies to many environmental interventions, as these are seeking to affect public goods, such as pollution control. With climate change, changes in behaviour are needed on the part of individual citizens to reduce carbon, by using cars less, changing levels of consumption of central heating or air conditioning, and so on. Even if many changes are not directly targeted at citizens, such as on packaging and materials for insulating homes, they need at base some degree of citizen consent or else they are not going to be popular and government will fear introducing them. There is a collective action problem with individual behaviours, such as people in Western countries thinking there is no point driving less when so many new cars are being driven in China (and vice versa).

Behaviours are hard to shift, because citizens might think it is the responsibility of those other than themselves, such as companies, elites, and governments of other countries, to take action. In addition, people are encouraged to consume more from society and to regard constraints on their behaviour as a loss of their rights, particularly if they can observe other classes or people in other countries as already consuming at a high level. It is also hard to address climate issues because of the slow rate of change and because people base their views on current weather, which may not be unfavourable. If people are not inclined to change their behaviour, confirmation bias may cause them not to select information that is relevant or provided from official sources. They read dire warnings from climate change experts, but still go on a pleasant day trip to the seaside or take a long-haul flight to an island that is about to be engulfed by rising sea levels caused by global warming.

THE IMPACT OF POVERTY

A big set of behavioural questions concern poverty, which is the consequence of a range of economic processes (World Bank 2015) and lack of resources. Just coping with poverty poses a large cognitive burden on individuals, which impinges on their ability to search for jobs and invest in long-run activities to help their families (Shafir and Mullainathan 2013). There is a further reason why poverty and poverty-reinforcing behaviours can have long-term effects. A variety of adverse environmental exposures during pregnancy and in early childhood can disrupt normal brain development and influence learning and acquiring behaviours. Such exposures include poor diet in pregnancy and recreational drugs (nicotine and alcohol), as well as maternal stress and anxiety, and are often linked with poverty. As the *World Development Report 2015* authors write, 'experiencing excessive stress and anxiety in infancy impairs the early development of learning abilities and non-cognitive skills, with cascading negative consequences for later achievements' (World Bank 2015: 101).

One mechanism thought to link early-life adversity to later-life outcomes concerns the phenomenon of epigenetics. Epigenetic marks such as DNA methylation and histone modification lie on top of the gene sequence (the inherited instructions for the organism) and play an important role in switching genes on or off, required for normal development and lifelong health. These marks are passed from cell to cell and sometimes from an individual to the individual's children – termed 'epigenetic inheritance'. While the genetic instructions passed on by parents to their children are not directly affected by the early environment, the epigenetic marks that control them can be (for an introduction to this subject, see Carey 2011). Epigenetic marks are particularly responsive to environmental factors during foetal development and early in childhood when the brain is developing most rapidly. This means that genes may not be correctly marked, and this abnormal marking may cause ill health later in life, with increased prevalence of mental health issues such as depression, anxiety and schizophrenia as well as metabolic disorders (see Kundakovic and Jaric 2017). Some studies suggest that incorrect marks can also be passed on down the generations, with even grandchildren affected by the environment of their grandparents. This means that poverty experienced in one generation can get locked into families, even when future generations might not experience so much poverty. Factors such as depression may affect the individual's ability to find and hold a job, to have sustained family relationships and to appropriately parent children, adding to adversity for the next generation. This process raises the question of whether intervention that improves the poverty of young mothers might prevent or even reverse incorrect epigenetic marks. Behaviour change interventions could create beneficial behaviours in young mothers during pregnancy and early motherhood aimed at reducing smoking or increasing healthy eating, which would benefit their own health and which could potentially have much longer-term beneficial consequences for their children by reducing the acquisition of incorrect epigenetic marks. It does suggest a large problem for policy-makers seeking to address the behaviours that reinforce poverty, as they face another hurdle, that of epigenetic causes of the behaviour, which come from the negative outcomes of that behaviour, so adding to self-reinforcing processes.

BLAME ATTRIBUTION

One area of great care when making the argument about the behavioural sources of policy outcomes is the attribution of responsibility to citizens when they do not bear the full responsibility for their actions or the consequences. At one level this is about actual causes, or the extent to which citizen action or inaction has caused the behaviour as opposed to other actors such as private firms or governments, and it is inevitably the case that all outcomes are multi-causal. There may be some responsibility, but other actors are also to blame. If the omission perspective is taken into account, then government and other actors could have been doing other things to put the situation right, so they bear responsibility for not following it through. The other aspect of this problem is that the actors interact in that each can shift blame on to the other as a reason for not acting. With the blame-shifting perspective there can be other reasons for inactivity, in that an opportunity for a cooperative relationship has been lost and outcomes become worse than they would have been if steps toward collective action had been taken. The solution is a partnership between government and citizens, which is often lost in a technocratic approach that assumes a tools or instrumental perspective to getting things done, or a social psychological perspective that regards behaviours as trapped within social structures and unchangeable. In fact, the capacity for citizens and bureaucrats to think differently can be an opportunity for change, but lack of capacity is itself a reason why behaviours are the source of negative policy outcomes and hard to break out of.

These arguments lead to a better understanding of the complex reasons for policy problems. These are to do with the system properties of both policy-making and human activity. Individuals behave according to their own inclinations, but also as social actors, so they respond to the signals and behaviours of friends and family and also to messages and incentives from organisations such as governments. This is the role of government as a regulator of the private sectors, and across a whole range of activities including the sector under consideration. In terms of health people may respond not just to their doctors and medical practitioners, but also to signals from those in education and from people in the private sector. There is a tendency for such social systems to tend to equilibrium, so all the actors feel no need to alter their behaviour, because the actions of the other players have caused them not to consider any changes. This can create poor outcomes that are reinforced by these supporting factors.

It is important to set out these causes of public policy problems, and not to assume that the behavioural aspect to public policy is purely a consequence of individual deficiencies. There are social causes for poor behaviours that get reinforced over time, and public agencies may compound these behaviours. This does not mean that nudgers should despair, but they need to realise the causes of the behaviours they wish to change and that individual behaviours are connected to many social processes and other government policies. Behaviours can be changed, but sustained behaviour change needs to be linked to other reforms and adjustments to standard operating procedures. Moreover, behaviours vary in their degree of embeddedness, with some behaviours relatively easy to shift, while others are more difficult. Policy-makers have seized on the easier-to-shift behaviours as a way to start the research agenda and to show the benefits of the nudge model. The greater challenge is to find out how to shift these more embedded behaviours.

CONCLUSION

Behaviour change is crucial for achieving positive outcomes for society, the economy, and politics, largely because behaviour contributes to human welfare, aggregating the actions of individuals for societal benefit. Change behaviour and individuals benefit, usually in the long term. As a result, there are collective gains in the form of reducing costs to the public purse, increasing the efficiency of the economy, and promoting a more agreeable and safe society for citizens to be part of. Other behaviours can enhance collective welfare without a great deal of benefit to the individual, which can be a harder problem to solve. The challenge is to change individual behaviours in combination with the decisions of others, so society may overcome collective action problems and individuals are incentivised to act for the public good. Overall, there are few public problems that could not be improved by changing individual behaviours, but public policy needs to be sensitive to the mechanisms causing those behaviours, and how they vary across domains.

In social science, there is a long and venerable tradition of understanding policy problems as a consequence of social and economic structures, such as power and inequality. Negative behaviours, such as in health, may often be seen as a consequence of structural factors, such as income inequality. The very reason behaviours are embedded, as discussed in this chapter, is often the result of long-term social and economic factors and even biology. These inequalities may be influenced by epigenetics, being shaped by the environment and then passed down the generations. There is a complex chain of causes and effects, which reformers should be aware of, and that includes behavioural public policy-makers. But those working on behaviour change do not ignore the important structural determinants of public policies. Behaviour change reformers wish to address what can be done in spite of the structural causes, by examining what choices individuals could make in certain situations, so as to get an advantage for themselves, or to understand a social or policy goal. These small changes may operate at the margin, maybe for only a few individuals, or just change outcomes in a small positive direction; but when summed over time and supported by repeated interventions, which may interact with other policy levers, they can lead to significant social improvements. Policy-makers can adopt a form of radical incrementalism to effect behaviour change over the long term (Halpern and Mason 2015).

That said, there is no doubt about the scale of challenge for policy-makers when addressing behaviour change, given the structural determinants of the problems, that so many aspects of behaviours are embedded into social networks, and the resistance people commonly display to any incentive or message that might cause them to change long-held habits. The question is whether an intervention has enough power or salience to effect behaviour change, whether it is meaningful for the individual and whether it can realistically be achieved. For that, reformers need a theory of behaviour change that is attuned to the psychological make-up of individuals so that government policy is more salient and can overcome internal barriers and hurdles. Such interventions need to address collective action problems, as individual behaviour links to other behaviours. Policy-makers therefore need a powerful theory to shape their interventions. The next chapter shows how behavioural economists have provided such a theory.

3. The behavioural revolution in the social sciences

It is important to start this chapter with the acknowledgement that the study of human behaviour is at the heart of social enquiry, a topic that appears in the first published thoughts about society, politics and the economy. As soon as intellectuals started thinking about society, they considered human behaviour as an important object of study. Social scientists in particular have sought to understand what drives human behaviour, right from the founders of sociology and economics, such as Emile Durkheim, who wanted to explain the prevalence of suicide in modern societies. Almost all forms of social inquiry involve a consideration of behaviour in some form, and even studies on what causes social and political attitudes entail a consideration of how those attitudes are affected by behaviour, which in turn affects attitudes. Yet there is something about the contemporary period that has heightened the academic interest; perhaps the prominence of the behavioural public problems highlighted in the last chapter has stimulated academics. Most importantly, researchers in the social sciences have managed to produce a more tractable set of theories and models that are of direct use outside the academy, which started from some esoteric research questions and models, of interest only to a handful of intellectuals, but which over time gradually developed into a larger body of knowledge.

This academic agenda is the field of behavioural economics. Over a short period of time, its ideas became influential and entered the mainstream of academic thinking, so laying the foundations for its later influence in public policy. In understanding the influence of nudge and behavioural public policy, it is important to find out how the ideas of behavioural economics emerged and why they took the course they did. This was not just the neutral process of scientific endeavour, but one where ideas came to prominence because they had found their right time and the appropriate context in which to emerge, and took a specific form because of the path dependency that affects the production of academic knowledge. The course the research took was influenced by an important debate within the discipline of economics about the veracity of rational actor models, which happened in spite of its two main protagonists,

Kahneman and Tversky, being psychologists. By being shaped within economics, the ideas emerged with a particular character and identity, which influenced how the whole subsequent research agenda in the behavioural sciences has developed, including the impact on public policy.

SOCIAL SCIENCE AND BEHAVIOUR CHANGE

Theories of individual behaviour are core to many disciplines and fields of enquiry, and occur in long-running research programmes that pre-date behavioural economics. Psychology as a discipline involves the study of human behaviour, often measured in the laboratory. A strong movement in psychology called 'behaviourism' stressed that human activity should be assessed by observing human behaviour (Skinner 1938), sometimes called 'radical behaviourism'. In political science, the term 'behavioural-ism' became a framework within which to carry out research on voting, participation, and interest group politics, addressing the family of behaviours that make up citizen and group involvement in politics, and was associated with the collection of systematic data, such as from surveys (see Sanders 2010).

The other social science activities that pre-date the behavioural public policy agenda were done in specialist fields linked to policy and professional practice, partly because of the employment by government of social scientists. Work in the field of health psychology looks at the utilisation of treatments and medicines and shows how individual cognition affects their success. It links closely with behavioural medicine, which seeks to alter the underlying behaviours leading to ill health. This discipline can trace its origins back to the start of the twentieth century, though in practice owes more to developments in the 1970s, such as the founding of the Society of Behavioral Medicine and the Academy of Behavioral Medicine Research.

Researchers in the social sciences have been interested in collecting data about behaviours without affecting the behaviour itself, such as through unobtrusive measures (Webb et al. 1966). Another long-running programme is research into design, which has influenced thinking about the design of buildings and engineering projects (Norman 1988). There is also a research field that examines how psychological factors affect the behaviour of road users, with a focus on what interventions might change that behaviour (e.g. Rothengatter and Groeger 1998). More generally, psychologists have long been interested in setting out models of human behaviour and in seeing how psychological theory can be

used to effect changes in public policy (Segall 1976). Another programme whose researchers are interested in the influence of messages on
human action is social marketing, which originates with consumer
research in the 1950s (Wiebe 1951–1952). It is a systemic attempt to
understand how to influence behaviours that have a wider social benefit
(Kotler and Zaltman 1971). This research area has expanded in recent
years, and its outputs can be found in specialist academic journals, such
as the *Journal of Social Marketing*. There are also a number of
prominent research institutes, such as the National Center for Health
Marketing at the Centers for Disease Control and Prevention (CDC), the
Social Marketing Institute (SMI) at Georgetown University and the
Institute for Social Marketing at the University of Stirling. Social
marketing is important for designing public information and promotion
campaigns to change behaviour (which was part of what nudge policies
were reacting against). As was discussed in Chapter 1, behavioural
economics differs through its focus on choice architectures and its more
direct attention to observed behaviour, but it is possible to observe
overlaps with research topics in social marketing, such as message
design (Tapp and Rundle-Thiele 2016). It should also be noted that
researchers in cognitive psychology have advanced knowledge of the
human brain, which did not affect the early work in behavioural
economics, but has now started to influence it and has become part of
the general intellectual flow of ideas. One example is psychological
work on cross-modal space, which is about the way in which sense
mechanisms interpret the world and give signals (see Spencer and Driver
2004). There are different parts of the brain that receive such messages,
which can be measured using scans. By understanding the neuro-
pathways, it may be possible to produce designs that appeal to particular
senses, such as designs of plates for suppressing hunger, as an aid to
diet. There is a wider set of applications, such as interventions that can
reduce smoking, which need careful designs to find out whether they are
effective (Varazzani 2017).

Health psychology, social marketing and brain sciences are all long-
running research programmes, which came about independently of the
current behavioural revolution, and continue in any case, inspiring the
agenda of behavioural public policy, and probably will carry on existing
irrespective of what happens to nudge and nudge units. In fact, researchers in these fields often think that those who advocate the new
behavioural agenda neglect existing research programmes and do not
give due credit to what has gone before. Nonetheless, what is interesting
about the current behavioural agenda is that it is more high-profile. It has

the ability to operate across disciplines, incorporate many sub-disciplines and be accepted by policy-makers and pundits. Nudge and behavioural public policy's prominence can increase the visibility of other research programmes, such as social marketing, and ensure the work of psychologists, who are employed in government or as part of official evaluations, is taken much more seriously. But the argument for the importance of behavioural economics is not just that it is a good label for a more psychological approach to understanding public policy, but that the approach blends psychology and economics in a novel way, which generates powerful insights for policy-makers.

THE RATIONAL MODEL

The reason why behavioural approaches are controversial owes much to debates within economics, which has a claim to be the dominant social science paradigm because of its link to and legitimation of wealth generation. Economists use mathematical models to theorise about economic relationships; these have a high degree of sophistication and their implications are tested using advanced statistics, creating traction in a world where scientific models hold sway in the generation of knowledge in the academy and in government.

The fundamental building block in economics is the concept of individual utility, which individuals seek to maximise through their choices. To understand the efficient selection of such choices, economists typically adopt a version of the rational model, where individuals have a clear objective to maximise, which is stable over time. Individuals can calculate the implications for realising their objective in terms of costs and benefits, and then can select the option that best meets it. The attraction of the model is that it offers micro-foundations for understanding human action in that individuals are seeking to realise preferences determined outside the economic model. There are system-level advantages in that individual welfare can be advanced by these choices, and can be aggregated for society as a whole through the expression of preferences and in market exchanges.

If individuals are assessing costs and benefits in making their decisions, then government policy can be adjusted to promote the collective benefit. Becker (1968) developed the economic approach to public policy when considering the costs and benefits of crime. Becker argued that, if people considering committing a crime rationally weighed up the costs and benefits, policy-makers could design a set of laws that could alter these costs and benefits. By changing penalties, certain kinds of crime could be reduced, for example. As a result of these guided choices, individual citizens would make decisions that in aggregate are closer to following the public interest. The model provides a clear justification for a paternalist approach to designing public policy, but it needs rational individual choices to be in play.

The power of the rational model is that it offers clear guidance to policy-makers about how to design a range of policies, not just laws and for crime, but across the whole gamut of tools of government and for any field. The model also tells decision-makers how to allocate public policies and finances efficiently. It reaches back to the utilitarian ideal that government is there to promote the greatest amount of happiness and welfare in society. By using its resources to alter costs and benefits, the politicians or bureaucrats can guide policy choices to improve welfare overall. Individuals reveal their preferences, and government can use these choices to produce beneficial outcomes. Given the complexity of public policy, it has an attractive simplicity that helps policy-makers solve problems.

A practical example helps understand how the economic model works. Imagine that the manager of a public housing estate has a small budget to prevent crime and has to make a choice about what to do with it, such as whether to invest in crime-prevention technology to stop break-ins, provide better street lighting to ensure people feel safe, or commission a public information campaign to increase the public's vigilance, or fund more street patrol to deter criminals. Using the rational model, the manager can decide to invest the budget on the basis of known calculations on the part of the residents of the estate and the likely activities of criminals. With a certain amount of expenditure on better window locks, some criminals may decide it is not worth the bother breaking in and decide to stay at home (or carry out the crime elsewhere). The manager can find out how much expenditure leads to a given reduction in crime; similarly, a certain amount of spending on lighting can change behaviour, and similarly with all the other measures, even expensive ones such as street patrols. The manager can then work out where to spend the fixed pot of money to the best effect, optimising the use of resources. The manager is being rational in allocating resources based on criminals being rational in responding to the incentives. And, to be clear, it is a behavioural model too, but one of a certain kind that the current generation of behavioural economists would wish to question or at least modify. However, it might be possible to keep a version of the rational model but incorporate biases on the part of citizens.

CRITIQUES OF THE RATIONAL MODEL

Recent studies of behaviour change modify the assumptions of the rational model, as they take into account human biases and heuristics when individuals assess information, although this insight is not particularly new. It goes back to the founders of economics. The older field of political economy operated with a complex account of individual behaviour (Oliver 2013a: 1), not least the insights of the classic theorists in political economy, such as Adam Smith, as well as earlier pioneers, such as Vernon Smith (Cartwright 2011: 5–9). In fact, the rational model was not fully present at the foundation of the study of economics, and was not developed until the neoclassical revolution of the late nineteenth century.

The focus on limits to rationality remains a core idea in psychology, in particular that human cognition has biases that prevent the rational weighing of options (see Sutherland 1992). Research on judgement that continues today in mainstream psychology (Newell et al. 2007). The critique of rational action has been very influential in other disciplines. It is possible to go back to the work of the influential administrative theorist Simon (1947) to find an attack on the rational model based on limited cognitive capacity. Simon offered a new model that shows how individuals follow informal decision-rules. They satisfice (that is take a course of action to get to a goal based on minimal cognitive effort) based on following past behaviours and economising on the costs of information searching. One can see the modern twist in the title of Simon's (1955) paper 'A behavioral model of rational choice'. Simon was very interested in using the research of psychologists to help him understand human behaviour, which linked to the research programme in the Carnegie School. Such ideas of the limited cognitions and bandwidth of human beings were central to the study of public administration, such as in the work of writers who saw an incremental pattern to human decision-making (Lindblom 1959), which influenced a generation of students in public policy and turns up in the language of today's behavioural policy-makers (Halpern and Mason 2015). Such a model underlies the influential book *Essence of Decision* (Allison 1971), about the Cuban missile crisis of 1962, in its critique of the rational actor and preference for an organisational process model. Even critics of incrementalism, such as Jones (1995), rely on a model that assumes that people vary in their attention to issues not in proportion to their actual threat, but in relation to the framing of the issue by the media and the feedback of many other influences, creating large shifts in policy, what are called 'policy punctuations'.

In spite of the influence of these models of human behaviour, they stayed largely within the academic study of public policy and public administration rather than in economics and other applied social sciences. The world of economics as it was put forward by the Chicago economists moved ahead from the 1950s with more sophisticated accounts of rational action. Rational choice models arguably became more visible in the 1980s as the rational foundations built into increasingly complex mathematical models. The world of evaluation and policy advice also became dominated by versions of the rational model, partly from the dominance of economics as a paradigm, and also from the elegant and practical way in which economic models helped policy-makers achieve their ends, such as through cost–benefit analysis.

It is important not to overstate the impact of a simple version of the rational model. As ever, the intellectual history is complex, with even a Chicago economist, Milton Friedman, questioning some assumptions of the rational model, as well as other paradoxes being discussed in the 1950s and 1960s (Oliver 2017: 16–30). Economists and others have usually been careful to claim that the rational model only offers a stylised version of human behaviour. It is a simplified model, and is not intended to be real. It should be used to clarify assumptions, to produce fresh accounts of social and economic processes, and to generate claims and predictions that can be tested in the real world in ways that lead to the formulation of more complex formal models (see Dowding and King 1995).

In spite of these careful claims, the rational model has been questioned or modified, as it is possible to question individuals' basic skills at solving problems or acting rationally, which concern the level of cognitive capacity involved. When supported by a framework of pre-existing choices, people might do fine in assessing them, but when faced with something new they do not perform so well. Relatively basic experiments show this, such as Schwartz's experiments on choice, whereby increasing the number of choices available, such as the number of brands of jam, makes individuals hardly able to make effective decisions (Schwartz

2005). Individuals may be thought of as 'scaffolded' by existing procedures and routines, which don't work at all well in new situations (Heath
and Anderson 2010: 233). The rational model might do fine to explain
marginal changes in stable situations in which individuals find themselves, but if the rules of the game change then individuals find it hard to
cope. Across a range of contexts, empirical tests of the basic propositions
of rational actor theories do not perform well. In political science, the
weight of the evidence for core political behaviours, such as voter
turnout, do not confirm the predictions from a simple rational choice
model (Green and Shapiro 1994). Other explanations of human behaviour
need to come into play to account for voter choice, even though it may
involve elements of rational calculation. Rational explanations and formal
models do not necessarily fall by the wayside; nor do behavioural
findings hinder the application of formal models to understand human
behaviour, as they can incorporate human biases and mental short cuts.
However, what is produced is a more nuanced and context-driven account
of human behaviour, where rational action plays a part but needs to be
integrated with a behavioural approach.

THE FOUNDING OF BEHAVIOURAL ECONOMICS

The development and current prominence of the psychological approach
in economics and public policy owe much to the work of Kahneman and
his collaborator Tversky (see Kahneman 1973, 2011; Kahneman and
Tversky 1979; Kahneman et al. 1982), whose work over several decades
influenced a large amount of research in economics and public policy
(see Lewis 2016). The scale of their influence is partly because they
worked for a long period of time in this field doing a series of
experiments that gradually added to knowledge. Importantly, they published some of their work in top economics journals, and also worked
closely with or communicated with leading economists, so influenced
thinking from within the world of rational choice models rather than
from outside. Their work was never seen as a threat to the old orthodoxy,
more as adding stimulation and challenge. Partly for this reason, Kahneman won the Nobel Prize for Economics in 2002, which both reflected
and consolidated his reputation. Jones et al. (2013: 10), citing Sent
(2004), argue that the reason that Kahneman and colleagues got such
recognition was because they spoke the language of rational thinking,
which was their starting point, rather than working with a completely
different intellectual framework. Oliver's (2017) history of behavioural

ideas in economics shows that economic theorists in the 1950s had already made a number of tweaks and modifications of rational models by exploring paradoxes, which made economists receptive to ideas from psychology.

As psychologists, Kahneman and Tversky worked on the field called 'judgement and decision-making'. They developed the influential prospect model whereby individuals overweight losses and underweight gains because of the psychological process at work (Kahneman and Tversky 1979). Significantly their paper was published in the prominent economic journal *Econometrica* and was set out in terms accepted by economists, in particular in equation form. Their approach links strongly to the endowment effect, which seeks to explain why people tend to trade much less than economic theory predicts (Thaler 1980; Kahneman et al. 1990). People value things just because they own them and do not want to lose them.

Tversky and Kahneman (1974) also developed the important term in behavioural economics of 'anchoring', which shows how the way in which information is provided, in particular the content of the first piece of information, influences current choices. They carried out a series of experiments that show that even people schooled in statistics were not able to solve basic arithmetic tasks. Another common term used in this field is 'mental accounting', which captures the limits people face when trying to calculate decisions which are quite complex in their heads and where biases creep in through the use of short cuts. People tend to think in relative terms rather than absolutely when considering these decisions (Thaler 1999). They will treat money in terms of its use or its origin, making decisions based on where it came from or where it is going rather than in absolute terms. Money is not seen as fungible, so people might treat a small win as cash to be spent, but a large win will be saved in total. Even experienced statisticians tend to focus on results which could not be supported by the data, believing in findings that were generated from small numbers that could not be generalised (Tversky and Kahneman 1971).

What is striking about Kahneman and colleagues' work is the care in the way it has been advanced, over a long period of time, which may have masked the underlying radicalism of the ideas, and maybe they even hid the radicalism from themselves. It was in the course of a long personal friendship, as Lewis's (2016) history recounts, that their ideas developed gradually. They questioned some of the axioms of economics, those that form into the rational actor model. These ideas and heuristics disrupt the framework of economic policy and undermine the assumptions behind claims of welfare efficiency. Economics assumes stable preferences, but in their work preferences may be shaped by short-run considerations and how issues are framed. As a result, many of the predictions of economic models are disrupted. However, the way the behavioural agenda unfolded did not highlight these radical implications, partly because academic work in economics had already anticipated them.

Moreover, behavioural economics does not need to be inconsistent with self-organised efficiency, as envisaged in the neoclassical model. Sugden (2004) shows that it is still possible to have efficiency even if contracts take place between non-rational consumers. Unstable or incoherent preferences can still yield efficient outcomes. Maybe because relaxing basic assumptions is a familiar procedure in economic analysis, behavioural economics can slip into the mainstream without much controversy. Ironically, the influence of Kahneman and Tversky in psychology has been more muted, with psychologists questioning the findings of some studies through the failure to replicate them, such as some of the priming studies (Engber 2016), though in fact the studies that are hard to replicate are mainly those reported in *Thinking, Fast and Slow* (Kahneman 2011) rather than the original experiments Kahneman carried out with Tversky.

BEHAVIOURAL ECONOMICS ENTERS THE MAINSTREAM

In the 1980s and 1990s, influenced by the work of Kahneman and Tversky, and other founders, such as Thaler, a new generation of behavioural economists started work on discovering how biases complicate economic models. These ideas gained momentum in the 1980s and 1990s. The movement started out in the work of a small circle of scholars, who benefited from their location in elite US universities, and the support of influential institutions, such as the Russell Sage Foundation. These scholars brought in younger students, who became the new vanguard. It was a quiet revolution, where the links between psychology and economics were gradually formed, as Thaler describes in his account of the making of behavioural economics (Thaler 2015). In small gatherings and through exchanges of papers, Kahneman was able to challenge directly some of the assumptions of economics, such as in his Asian disease test (Tversky and Kahneman 1981), presented in front of influential economists (Thaler 2015: 159–160). Thaler was invited to contribute a regular column, 'Anomalies', to the *Journal of Economic Perspectives* (later collected in his 1994 book *The Winner's Curse*).

Rabin's (1998) paper on psychology and economics makes the case for behavioural economics most strongly and points out the challenges, in weak and strong form, to economic theory in general (see also DellaVigna 2009). The objective was to introduce psychological realism behind economic models as a way that improves them rather than to overthrow the project and methods of the discipline of economics. Economics remains characterised by methodological individualism, formal or mathematical models that build from assumptions, and then careful tests of the implications of these models using advanced statistics, all of which remain in place in behavioural economics.

As time went by, models of individual behaviour became more sophisticated. Theories of inter-temporal choice, which are about the making of a decision and understanding the consequences of it over time, have been important (Ainslie 1975; see the review by Berns et al. 2007). Such choices are subject to bias, and hence what is called 'hyperbolic discounting', which can be specified mathematically, and these papers again appear in top economics journals (e.g. Ainslie 1991). More informally, experiments can show that people make choices based in heuristics about whether to accept a sum of money now or a different sum later, which generally show a preference for a more immediate but smaller sum now. Such lack of control is largely seen as the reason why savings do not take place as much as conceived in classical economic theory (see Harris and Laibson 2002).

Another concept that was developed at this time was 'preference reversal', which was formulated by Tversky and Thaler (1990), though was already set out in the work of Grether and Plott (1979). The concept tries to account for why people change behaviours, revealing different preferences during the course of making choices, which often follow from the procedural set-up of those choices, influenced by the scales and units people face. As with other concepts in behavioural economics, a research programme has been set off, with the idea being developed by academics such as Loewenstein (1987) and List (2002).

These studies formed part of a more general movement in economics, whose members started to use field experiments to test real-world interventions, moving away from laboratory experiments (see Levitt and List 2007; Banerjee and Duflo 2014). This shift from using the more psychological methods of the laboratory to field experiments has important consequences, as the following chapters indicate. Behavioural economists had started to engage policy problems through testing interventions which were still interesting theoretically but also tried out policy initiatives in the real world.

A key idea that also had implications beyond the academy was of status quo bias and inertia. This is the idea that, if people want to conserve cognitive energy, they might simply choose the status quo option, which may mean no change in behaviour even when it is clearly in their interests to change, and of course links to the heuristics approach discussed earlier. It also follows from Kahneman's idea of loss aversion as a reason why it might be better to stick with the status quo, as it does not entail risk, or at least the perception of risk. Thaler was a notable exponent of this concept, as he was the co-author of a famous article by Kahneman et al. (1991). Even the original article, published in an eminent journal, was to an extent homespun, with its starting example of a friend's wine-buying decision. The default option is introduced, again in easy-to-understand examples of offers made by an electric power company and US state laws on car insurance. The authors argue for the importance of these findings by saying they violate the assumptions of stable preferences, yet the style is not aggressive and rests on reasonableness and plausibility, as well as logical argument and evidence. As well as conservatism, people suffer from overconfidence or optimism bias, so they overstate their skills and make rash decisions (Sunstein 2014a: 48). The tendency to come up with a range of propositions that appear to contradict each other is one of the characteristics of behavioural sciences. Rather than elaborating a general theory, research seeks to find the exact context in which a psychological trait will have an effect on decision-making.

CHANGES IN MAINSTREAM ECONOMICS

At the same time as these behavioural concepts were being developed, scholars in other branches of economics started to look at the impact of human-centred motivations that do not strictly follow the rational model. In tests of the propositions of game theory, it had started to be accepted that players do not choose options that benefit themselves, but are prepared to share the proceeds (e.g. Camerer 2003). Economists started to accept that individuals display altruism in their dealings with others and that they like to reciprocate, which forced theorists to modify the rational model. These findings can be complemented by the way in which economists acknowledge the idea that individuals may trust each other in ways that do not follow the predictions of the tragedy of the commons or prisoner's dilemma games. This body of evidence from laboratory experiments on game theory is reviewed in Ostrom's (1997) address to the American Political Science Association, which essentially says that a behavioural approach is needed to understand how collective action works rather than the predictions of the prisoner's dilemma game. As Cartwright writes, 'game theory was instrumental in the birth of behavioural economics' (2011: 9). This influence was because revisions to the standard economic model were first explored in the laboratory, then economists started to test such propositions in the field, for example Gneezy and List's (2006) investigation of gift exchange in labour markets. That Ostrom, a political scientist, won the Nobel Prize for economics is also evidence about the change in direction within the discipline, which of course does not mean that fundamental ways of understanding the world and core methods have been overthrown in economics, but that the discipline had broadened out to take on board non-economic motivations, which then form part of its intellectual project. Some of these themes were already buried in arcane debates and papers, but they were ready to be rediscovered.

Behavioural economics fits well with this non-radical reorientation of the discipline, which has the consequence of protecting economics from criticism and preparing it for a more challenging period, following the certainties of the 1980s and 1990s, after the financial crash of 2008. In this way, economics broadened out so as to retain its distinctiveness and ensure its intellectual superiority through formal modelling, and the use of advanced statistical methods to test the implications from the models.

THE SOPHISTICATION OF BEHAVIOURAL ECONOMICS

Consistent with the mainstreaming of behavioural economics is the greater use of formal models and the increased sophistication of the tests applied. For example, Park and Sabourian (2011) use complex mathematical models to understand herding in financial markets, which can help explain their instability. More recent developments show the power of behaviourally inspired economics to offer a more integrated account of how the economy works, which is shown by a recent move to behavioural macroeconomics, which harks back to Keynes's model, but is fully updated and enhanced with the insights of behavioural economics (see Akerlof 2002; Gabaix 2016). The macroeconomic model includes behavioural findings on savings and the behaviour of asset markets. It uses concepts from behavioural economics, such as loss aversion, which can then feed into macroeconomic models.

Another route to advancing behavioural economics is through greater understanding of individual psychology, between aspects of individual behaviour that focus on planning and other inclinations to be a doer or to act out of habit. This again is a neat way to retain aspects of rational actor models, but to suggest that behaviour is contingent and may depend on prompts. So why do people procrastinate when they know that acting immediately will benefit them and save the costs of procrastination (Anderson 2016)? Then there is Thaler's planner and doer framework, whereby individuals might not be able to exercise self-control (Thaler and Shefrin 1981), so they may need a device or a commitment to help them achieve their goals. A similar idea appears in Kahneman's (2011) more recent work of synthesis, that of two systems of thinking: system 1 is fast, instinctive and done with gut feelings; system 2 is more considered, deliberative and slower. Understanding these two systems provides a route to understanding the general operation of individual psychology in economics and is a way to understand generally how bias operates at times to modify the assumptions of an earlier generation of economic theorists. But it is also fair to say that, even though these approaches are highly attractive intuitively and one can imagine individuals moving between the kinds of thinking – planner and doer – of the two systems, there is no meta-theory that tells us when to expect transitions from one approach to another, so there is no predictive integrative model that can guide the whole system. This means that behavioural economics broadens out to make predictions that are contingent rather than universal. Given that behavioural economics tends to use ideas from psychology rather than innovate itself, it tends to replicate psychology's tendency to subdivide processes into many different causal mechanisms and heuristics, which can become very numerous as different traits are identified and then given their respective labels. In this way, which is not stated, behavioural economics is slightly different to the classical variety in spite of sharing the basic approach, in that classical economics built up its understanding of economic relationships from micro-foundations. The elegance of economic theory gets complicated in its behavioural variant.

ACADEMIC APPROACHES TO POLICY PROBLEMS

As well as pursuing theoretical developments, behavioural economics started to address policy problems in concrete areas, which is entirely consistent with the grounded way in which behavioural economists think about the world and the general programme of behavioural economics, which is to find contexts where specific mechanisms explain human behaviour. Even in advanced economics papers, there are often policy prescriptions.

Thaler and Benartzi (2004) have pioneered this practical focus by examining pensions choice, testing whether defaults encourage employees to sign into a pension scheme. The authors carried out interventions with private sector companies to see if the default option and giving the default at the same time as a pay rise would encourage people to make savings for a pension, as a way of addressing people's bias in not wanting to forgo their current earnings. The promising results are useful tests of status quo bias, but also have a practical application. Another example is taxation, whether making local sales taxes more salient affects consumer behaviour, which has been tested experimentally (Chetty and Saez 2013). Health is another big area, such as in the work of Loewenstein et al. (2013) on the lack of public understanding of health insurance. Formal work has looked at the question of moral hazard in the purchase of health insurance, and that there is a human tendency to undervalue health as a result. There are policy implications of adjusting co-payment and of adjusting the nudges to respond to perceptions of behavioural hazard (Baicker et al. 2015).

THE DIFFUSION OF BEHAVIOURAL ECONOMICS

The final set of developments has been the expansion of the ideas of behavioural economics into other disciplines, which makes the research programme genuinely interdisciplinary. One key area is law, whose scholars took an early interest (Sunstein 2000), and which has developed into a subfield of its own (Zamir and Teichman 2014; Alemanno and Sibony 2015), which is about the reach and effectiveness of legal instruments, and also concerns legal argument about giving reasons and justifying autonomy (see Chapter 7). Other developments are the study of behavioural public policy, which is the investigation of how behavioural instruments can have an influence on policy outcomes (Oliver 2013a). There is behavioural public administration, which is based on making a closer link between psychology and public administration, and is designed to help scholars better understand bureaucratic behaviour (Tummers et al. 2016). Development economists have embraced behaviour change theories and evidence, as shown by the World Bank (2015) report cited earlier.

CONCLUSION

This review of behavioural economics, as well as studies of human behaviour in other parts of the social sciences, shows a remarkable set of intellectual developments. What has happened is that the hegemony of rational actor models in economics, and in other disciplines, has lessened, and alternative accounts of motivations for human behaviour have become more commonly articulated and accepted. The argument in this chapter has sought to acknowledge the pedigree of psychological approaches to understanding human behaviour and the long-standing critique of rational actor models, which have been conventional wisdom in the study of public policy, in work going back to the 1940s. But the key feature of the current period of debate, which has been more in evidence since the late 1970s, has been its occurrence inside or proximate to the discipline of economics.

It has been a quiet revolution, happening over many decades. It has been easier than might have been expected, because economists have always discussed different kinds of theoretical models and have been open to puzzles and contradictions. Economists usually stress that their models depend on simplifying assumptions so as to facilitate mathematical modelling, rather than believing the assumptions are necessarily true, as they are often designed to be relaxed at a later stage. Partly for these reasons, key papers in behavioural economics appeared in the key academic journals in the discipline, such as the *American Economic Review*, and were written by faculty in high-ranking departments, such as from the universities of Princeton and Chicago. The economics mainstream matured gradually in this period, with economists taking more of an interest in motivations and findings that arise outside the assumptions of the rational model, producing theories and research on new topics such as trust, reciprocity, and altruism, and discussing the mental processes that behavioural economists had uncovered. Economics has broadened out to incorporate this line of thinking in a way that runs alongside or is in dialogue with research using the rational actor model, reflecting the hidden depths of the discipline as a whole. In the process, economics retains its distinctive contribution by formalising the propositions that behavioural economists have put forward and testing them using advanced statistical methods. This integration of behavioural models into the mainstream is an important development, given the importance of economics in the hierarchy of forms of knowledge, which is accepted in the academy and reinforced in the public sphere. Given the legitimacy of economics, this prominence helped researchers outside economics take the concept of biased behaviours more seriously. Some of those outside the discipline who adhered to a version of the rational model could see how it could be adapted in line with the findings of behavioural economics; others who were more critical could say that they had been proved right all along. But it was not the case that economics lessened in its dominance in the academy and in the public sphere; in fact, the opening up of economics ensures its continuing dominance and legitimacy, reinforced rather than undermined by these new ideas.

The redefinition of economics was to have a large effect on the public realm. As it became more realistic, while remaining rigorous, the possibility was for a wide-ranging influence on how researchers and academics sought to improve public policy outcomes through public action, developments that the next chapter teases out.

4. Nudge: All tools are informational now

Behavioural sciences and behavioural economics have entered the mainstream, at first within academic disciplines, but more profoundly within the world of media debate and commentary, and thence into the ambit of policy-makers. As will be documented in this chapter, this translation is an important development, a case study of how an academic programme can directly influence public policy. This phenomenon is not automatic. Indeed, the conventional wisdom is that academics find it hard to make a direct impact (e.g. Caplan 1975, 1979), for example through official evaluations. It is only when there are special conditions in place that academics can position themselves to affect policy choices (see John 2013b). Academics need to understand that it is mainly through the propagation of ideas that they can have a profound influence (Weiss 1977), which is gradual and long-lasting, and this is the realm in which advocates of behavioural economics so successfully operate.

The success of behavioural public policy derives in part from the practical agenda of behavioural economics itself, discussed in the last chapter, which is because of the realism that the introduction of psychology entailed. It helped the consideration of policy questions within academic research projects. The salience and impact of the new sets of ideas came from the synthesis of economics and psychology that modified rational actor models. As a result of the research programme that emerged, academics soon realised that they had discovered a powerful set of tools, which were capable of shifting behaviours with relatively few inputs, so addressing the behavioural concerns discussed in Chapter 2, but without implying large contributions from government resources. The other reason for success is that the advocates of behavioural economics were good translators of the science into claims and propositions that could be easily understood. This chapter is about this translation, and shows skilful advocacy by the proponents of behaviour change, who simplified the propositions, created eye-catching summaries, and made the behavioural cues seem just like common sense. In fact, they used all the skills of nudge to sell nudge itself.

THE SIMPLIFICATION OF BEHAVIOURAL ECONOMICS

Many behavioural economists are talented advocates, not really needing other translators. They are persuasive characters, used to the public world of US elite universities, with their easy access to the op-eds of the *New York Times* and the *Washington Post*. The findings they convey are appealing because they are often based on easy-to-understand tests or experiments. Taking pot shots at a simple version of the rational model, replacing it with smart pieces of research that reveal a more human side, especially for everyday activities and routines, is a good sell for the quality newspaper market. For example, Johnson and Goldstein's (2003) seminal study on organ donations, which showed the importance of a default, was published in a general science journal, which helped get the results noticed. Thaler was instrumental in this process of dissemination, which may have come from his relaxed and convivial personality. He is known for making colourful asides and wry jokes, commenting on human frailties, and peppering his talks and prose with funny but apposite anecdotes. It is no surprise that the pensions default example should have become so well known, and been communicated so effectively to policy-makers (see Thaler 2015: 314), for example in a contribution to the policy forum in *Science* (Benartzi and Thaler 2013). Benartzi is a persistent advocate, who did his own publicity-seeking tours and gave the obligatory TED talks. He published an advocacy book (Benartzi 2012) on pensions choice, as well as having a website and a consultancy. Of course, Thaler made great play of pensions defaults in his co-authored nudge book (Thaler and Sunstein 2008).

POLICY-MAKERS AND THE BEHAVIOURAL AGENDA

Before discussing the nudge book (Thaler and Sunstein 2008), it is important to emphasise that the findings of behavioural economics were reaching outside the academy during the 1990s, as findings started to emerge and discussion was taking place in the circles that Thaler (2015) discusses so well in his book *Misbehaving*. The pensions example has already been mentioned. The *New York Times* celebrated the arrival of behavioural economics as early as 2001 (Uchitelle 2001), mentioning the work of David Laibson and hyperbolic discounting. The winning of the Nobel Prize by Kahneman in 2002 generated much commentary (see Altman 2002).

Academics were not the only ones doing the translating. The classic intermediators were those working for think tanks and policy institutes who like to sift through the vast output of academic journals, find out what research is hot, and then do literature reviews. In the UK, the New Economics Foundation commissioned such a study. Shah and Dawney (2005) produced their seven principles, which the authors had divined from reading the literature reviewed in the previous chapter. They distilled the findings into a list: other people's behaviour matters; habits are important; people are motivated to do the right thing; people's self-expectations influence how they behave; people are loss-averse and hang on to what they consider theirs; people are bad at computation when making decisions; and people need to feel involved and effective to make a change. Lists have been important for the diffusion of behavioural economics, and comes from the way in which they draw attention to particular cognitive processes, and reflect the relative weakness (or advantage, depending how it is seen) in not having an integrative theory. Weakness in the pantheon of knowledge can be a strength in the world of diffusing ideas, because lists are less threatening, and it is possible for the reader to focus on one or two claims that are appealing rather than feel a need to accept the programme wholesale. In particular, the subtitle of Shah and Dawney's (2005) publication, *Seven Principles for Policy-Makers*, makes it clear the audience is people who make decisions in the public realm. Each section of the publication has a subsection on relevance to policy-makers. At the same time, and this is another characteristic of this new applied field of enquiry, the publication refers directly to academic studies, giving the title of papers and directly referencing them, for example Frey et al.'s (2004) review of procedural utility, the idea that a sense of procedural fairness encourages people to comply, published in what for policy-makers must seem a fairly obscure academic journal. The publication is replete with summaries of such academic reviews, with academics doing the summaries, which are in turn summarised by people who work in the policy world, as this needs different skills of translation. This simplification of academic work makes it more easily digestible, and it needs a particular aptitude, as communicating and summarising the results of academic research require different abilities to those needed to publish an academic article (see Flinders 2013). The main question to ask is whether the simplification loses something of the potency of the ideas, as these documents tend to concentrate on the less threatening proposals.

The Strategy Unit in the Cabinet Office, under prime minister Tony Blair, commissioned its own report on behavioural economics. Blair had hired Halpern (see Halpern 2015) to work in the unit. He had become known for his work on social capital, and he had absorbed insights on behaviour change. He has a background in social psychology, but also worked directly with policy-makers in the Options for Britain project (Halpern et al. 1996), which reviewed policy options shortly before the 1997 election, and in Nexus, the online think tank. Halpern appears later as the director of the Behavioural Insights Team (BIT). Working for Blair, Halpern and colleagues produced a report looking at the policy options from research on human behaviour (Cabinet Office – Prime Minister's Strategy Unit 2004). The report begins with the importance of behaviour for policy (similar to the argument articulated in Chapter 2). Central to the report is a section on theories of behaviour change, which contains reviews of the rational actor model. Tversky and Kahneman are cited alongside other key authors. Then appear key concepts in behavioural economics, such as scarcity, availability, and prospect theory, with the terms 'loss' and 'gain', referring to the classic paper by Kahneman et al. (1990). For a government report, there is much use of academic terms, such as 'fundamental attribution error' and 'social cognitive theory'. As Halpern discusses (2015: 30), the report met with controversy; but it illustrates how close the relationship between the academy and government had become, with Kahneman visiting the Cabinet Office in this period (Halpern 2015: 32).

At the same time, other parts of UK central government produced reviews of behaviour change research. Government Social Research (GSR), which coordinated research across government, commissioned a report, published in 2008, which looked at the literature on behavioural economics (Darton 2008), as well as producing a practical guide. Defra, the former environment and farming ministry, produced a series of research reports, which were essentially literature reviews of the behavioural science literature (Pike et al. 2010).

THE NUDGE BOOK

The book by Thaler and Sunstein, *Nudge: Improving Decisions about Health, Wealth, and Happiness* (2008), is the ultimate exercise in translation. The argument is that policy-makers can be choice architects: they can influence the choices people make by redesigning procedures and institutions in ways that privilege socially beneficial outcomes. Choice architects can take advantage of the argument that people tend to choose the status quo or default option, which of course comes out of status quo bias claims in the behavioural economics literature. People tend to be cognitive misers, maybe even lazy, so they tend to go for the easiest option or one that does not entail any change. In many circumstances, the no-change option can be the least beneficial. People end up defaulting to choices that benefit them the least, such as no pension scheme or a poor insurance renewal policy, and/or one from which society does not benefit (e.g. not donating organs). But what if government could organise procedures and rules so that the default option was the one that had the most personal and societal benefit, such as the best pension or insurance scheme, or where donating organs was the default activity for anyone renewing a car licence?

The nudge aspect is the idea that such interventions are light-touch; that is, they guide individuals to where they want to go or would want to go if they gave the option enough thought, but does not force them, enabling people to keep their liberty intact. The interventions still act paternalistically, which is captured by the apparently oxymoronic term 'libertarian paternalism', which will be discussed in Chapter 7. Keeping an element of freedom is key to Thaler and Sunstein's definition of nudge:

> any aspect of the choice architecture that alters people's behavior in a predictable way without forbidding any options or significantly changing their economic incentives. To count as a mere nudge, the intervention must be easy and cheap to avoid. Nudges are not mandates. Putting fruit at eye level counts as a nudge. Banning junk food does not. (Thaler and Sunstein 2008: 6)

The focus is on choice and how policy-makers respect the basic values and long-term preferences of those who are nudged.

The nudge book (Thaler and Sunstein 2008) walks the reader through other terms in behavioural economics, such as 'anchoring', 'availability', 'overconfidence', 'gains', and 'losses', yet again showing the love of lists in behavioural public policy. As the book unfolds, examples and case studies appear from the world of investment, organ donations, energy saving, and many others, ending up with a recommendation for a dozen nudges, so directly speaking to policy-makers. But what characterises the book the most is its lightness of tone, the humorous quips, the hint that it is Thaler who corresponds to the lazy person needing nudging, and then the pretend jostling between the authors, all of which sugars the behavioural public policy pill quite considerably. It was no surprise that the book was a hit, and the funnier of the two authors became a media star, especially in the UK. A phenomenon had been born, and a thousand nudge jokes set forth, the word entering the vocabulary of commentators and becoming something that policy-makers should think about doing. The book, with its eye-catching yellow elephant on the cover, appeared in newsagents and airport booksellers, the ultimate trade publication. The book and its positive reception then fed back into academia, which turned nudge into a veritable industry of new investigations, moving beyond the formulations of behavioural economics, more interested in how the rational model could be modified and formalised, into more direct tests of policy interventions. The question had become less about elaborating a psychological model of economic behaviour and more about finding out which psychological process would be best attuned to motivating human beings to act. The translation had happened.

THE WORLD OF PRACTITIONER GUIDES

In the wake of *Nudge*, a range of publications emerged, partly influenced by it, partly doing their own research. One was the popular MINDSPACE report (Hallsworth et al. 2010). As with the earlier Cabinet Office report on behaviour and policy, this piece of desk research emerged from the heart of the UK government machine, commissioned by the Cabinet Office, and this was still when Labour was in office, which shows that nudge in the UK pre-dated the Conservative–Liberal Democrat Coalition government. It partly reflects the enthusiasm of an unconventional and highly talented Cabinet secretary, Gus O'Donnell, Britain's leading civil servant, who was an academic economist and really liked the practical application of economics. Again, Halpern was involved, this time from outside government, based in the Institute for Government, as well as other researchers. It was a thorough review of the academic literature on behavioural economics, with copious references to research pieces in the academic journals, and had footnotes galore. But the key to the publication was the acronym MINDSPACE, which captures the importance of thinking about mental processes and represents different nudges that can be chosen depending on the situation policy-makers are faced with (again replicating the tendency of guides in behavioural public policy to produce lists of nudges). The acronym covers much of the ground of behavioural economics: messenger, incentives, norms, defaults, salience, priming, affect, commitments, and ego. The only one that appears to jar is incentives, as behavioural economists try to move away from a simple understanding of incentives (this is where the authors summon in losses, but presumably they needed a vowel to make the acronym work). The report, with its many examples, is attractive to policy-makers, but also has academic credibility (it ended up as a paper in an academic journal – see Dolan et al. 2012). MINDSPACE quickly became a hit, not as an airport book, but as a download (the Institute for Government's most accessed). The word, like nudge, has become common currency and, as will be shown in Chapter 5, is still used as a guide by which policy-makers could apply behavioural insights, in spite of attempts to displace it with other, shorter acronyms.

NUDGE GOES BACK TO THE ACADEMY

As was briefly discussed in Chapter 3, one impact of the greater policy interest has been the reorientation of the academy itself to focus on more concrete policy issues. Academics have always taken an interest in behavioural policies, but these applications tended to appear in specialist disciplines or field areas, such as the environment and health. What distinguishes the new field of interest is that it works across many fields and seeks to draw behavioural insights in a number of contexts, with the driving interest being the identification of the psychological cue. A new descriptor emerged, 'behavioural public policy', which denotes a more serious tone than the enterprise of nudge, and by implication a wider range of applications. In many ways academics are practising behavioural public policy in carrying out applied interventions that are of use to the policy world and in the academy. Advocates of this approach seek to ensure that insights from psychology predominate in understanding how policy interventions and bureaucratic routines work in practice.

Behavioural public policy became an option on master's courses (e.g. at the London School of Economics). It has been written about in the quality press. It is represented as part of the ambit of the Behavioral Science and Policy Association, which acts to translate findings from the behavioural sciences into policy. It is the title of a new journal published by Cambridge University Press (see https://www.cambridge.org/core/journals/behavioural-public-policy) and of an edited book (Oliver 2013a), the latter with contributions on environmental policy, health, and financial behaviour as well as more general applications. *The Behavioral Foundations of Public Policy* (Shafir 2013) is a more ambitious volume in the same vein, seeking to provide coverage across many theories and venues to show the potential for a structured and wide-ranging debate about the causes and remedies of behavioural public problems.

Some of these academic treatments were a conscious reaction to the agenda carved out by nudge, partly in praise of it but also keen to ensure that the terms of the debate remained open to a wide range of contexts whereby behavioural interventions could apply. Nudge implies that the space for behavioural interventions is where individuals have choice or autonomy. Individuals really wanted to do an activity, but through lack of attention or status quo bias did not do it. Several writers have questioned this limitation. John (2013a) argues that nudges apply across the tools of government and can be used to improve the informational context within which the tools of government are exercised. A tool of government, such as a tax change or a new law, might at first appear authoritative and capable of implementation only by virtue of the power of the state. But, as every student of implementation knows, an insight that goes back to Pressman and Wildavsky's (1973) famous study, the various levers and controls that a central authority can deploy are never fully going to work (see John 2011). There are too many complex chains of command and autonomous organisations that need to work together. The way to achieve better implementation is to improve the information environment when using the tools, which can help their effectiveness, such as the clear or socially-informed communication of a new law or tax change.

What the nudge agenda adds is a close understanding of how a law or tool is going to apply in behavioural terms. It can be redesigned so as to work better, but in keeping with the choices and wishes of the person or organisation involved. This is because a key part of responding to government policy is the understanding and appreciation of the salience of signals, which can vary in the extent to which they offer an impetus to change behaviour. In this way, 'All tools are informational now' (John 2013a). Oliver (2013b) makes a similar argument, but he is interested in the extent to which a policy change involves regulation or not. Non-regulation is the world of nudge; but the world of regulation, which can still use behavioural insights, is called 'budge' so as to distinguish it from non-obtrusive measures, such as the defaults in the Thaler and Sunstein (2008) formulation. In this way, the debate about behavioural public policy, behaviour change, and nudge is an expanding canvas designed to be the academic study of policy effects, that is decisions taken by policy-makers to change outcomes using procedures and tools of government to achieve their ends. Essentially, this is a literature about evaluation, about the possibility of achieving changes in policy outcomes, albeit grounded in behavioural sciences and theory. The tools approach shows that nudge can deal with the core problems in public policy rather than just be about improving communications. The chains of implementation can be examined using behavioural concepts, identifying the precise mechanisms that can help make a policy work. Making those chains work in better ways can then foster a spirit of innovation that infuses the whole delivery process to make it more efficient and responsive. This wide-ranging ambition not to leave any stone unturned becomes part of the radical agenda for nudge that this book takes up in later chapters.

In tandem with nudge, work that uses ideas from psychology, particularly in health, had also started to be simplified, creating guides for policy-makers and others, maintaining a bridge between academia and the policy world. Influential has been the behaviour change wheel, which is a heuristic device invented by Michie and colleagues (Michie et al. 2011), who desk-reviewed a series of frameworks on behaviour change and synthesised them into a framework, which was first promoted in academic articles, then with the website and book, with a focus on influencing practitioners. It uses the COM-B ('capability', 'opportunity', 'motivation' and 'behaviour') model to make a rounded assessment of what tools to use and what potential they have. These tools are called 'intervention functions', and relate to the tools of government literature discussed earlier. The different fields are represented as a wheel, with processes and tools of government placed in successive circles so observers can select which choice or set of choices is appropriate for the situation they face. The wheel becomes an aid to decision-making, but one rooted in academic knowledge. It probably appeals most to those who work on health policy interventions, where there is a stronger grounding of academic ideas and common use of ideas from academic psychology, but the guide is more complex than many of the other simplifications.

THE WIDER PHENOMENON OF TRANSLATION

The torrent of publications and outlets of behavioural public policy need to be seen as part of the wider phenomenon of translation of findings from the academy into practice. This transfer had always happened, and right from the start of social science there have been those who have written about the findings of the academy in an attractive style. The eminent think tank Chatham House was founded in the 1920s. The social affairs think tank Political and Economic Planning was founded in 1931, and went on to become the research organisation Policy Studies Institute (PSI). In the US, the Brookings Foundation, which has a wide public policy remit, was founded in 1916. Think tanks provide this role of translation by providing summaries and inviting academics to present their findings to policy-makers, and have generally been regarded as being influential in the policy process, in particular in helping shifts in ideas (Stone 1996). And so it has been the case with behavioural economics. In fact, it is possible to argue that the translation phenomenon has become an industry in recent years, which has benefited the behavioural sciences. Funding councils and foundations have helped too with their focus on ensuring impact as a condition of grant funding, and with governments, such as that of the UK, enshrining policy relevance in their evaluation of the outputs of higher education institutions, for example the Higher Education Funding Council for England's (HEFCE) Research Excellence Framework (REF).

The role of academics simplifying their findings into a book that is readable goes back to the paperback revolution of the 1960s, if not before. In fact, Adam Smith's *An Inquiry into the Nature and Causes of the Wealth of Nations* ([1776] 1904) is sometimes regarded as a piece of translation, although it is the age of cheap publishing and business books that has seen the explosion. Of course, popular psychology has always been important. Economics was a latecomer in spite of Keynes and Galbraith's early entries in this field. Since the mathematical strides of the 1980s, there has been a swing back to the more practical concerns, which has led to this spate of books. An example is *Freakonomics* (Levitt and Dubner 2005), which sought to summarise examples of applications of economics to solve policy problems, with state-of-the-art research methods and designs (explained simply), often with counterintuitive conclusions and recommendations. There have been sequels to this book, a website with resources to read, and a regular podcast for listeners to download. Of course, some of the insights in *Freakonomics* come from behavioural economics broadly considered.

More directly behavioural is the book *Scarcity: Why Having Too Little Means So Much*, which summarises research on the impact on behaviours of scarcity, in particular the impact of poverty, which narrows the range of choices families can make because of the pressure on cognitions (Shafir and Mullainathan 2013). The book's authors translate this work through the consultancy Ideas42 (see http://www.ideas42.org), whose aim is to 'to use the power of behavioural science to design scalable solutions to some of society's most difficult problems'. Of particular prominence is Ideas42, which reflects a general trend in the dissemination of behavioural ideas, which is using behavioural insights to seek to solve problems of implementing interventions in developing countries, for example ensuring the behavioural insights apply to the uptake of financial services so that individuals understand the risks involved, or advocating interventions such as pensions defaults. Reflecting this interest in using behavioural insights, the World Bank (2015) commissioned one of its research projects on 'Mind, Society, and Behavior'. The report has chapters on poverty and development, household finance and climate change. It makes the case strongly for using a more psychologically attuned account of human behaviour rather than the standard economic model (see Demeritt and Hoff 2015). Behavioural economists have piled in too, such as Gneezy and List (2013), whose *The Why Axis: Hidden Motives and the Undiscovered Economics of Everyday Life* is an account of how incentives operate in broad and social ways.

Such diffusion can be seen in other fields too. For the environment, Jackson (2005) reviews sustainable lifestyles, using the tools of behavioural science, though coming to some cautious conclusions about what may be possible in the environmental field given the entrenched nature of the behaviours to shift. Another big area for behavioural insights is design. Architects can use these ideas to reshape public spaces, such as walkways and public housing estates, which can be seen as part of a more ethnographic approach to understanding organisations (Kimbell 2015). Similarly, academics who work in the field of social marketing find their ideas being used as ways to promote behaviour change by consultancies, such as the National Social Marketing Centre (see http://www.thensmc.com/what-social-marketing).

Journalists have contributed to the popularisation of behavioural economics, for example the *Financial Times* journalist Tim Harford. His books on economic problems and solutions (e.g. Harford 2005), newspaper column, and BBC Radio 4 programme *More or Less*, which he presents, contain many examples from behavioural economics. The large number of science policy writers have also contributed to the debate. In these popular science books is the idea that the evidence base matters, such as from the use of experiments. People who write about science believe that scientific methods should have a wider application in public policy (Henderson 2012). A similar approach is taken by the critic of the use of trials in medicine, Ben Goldacre, a doctor who takes the pharmaceutical companies to task for poor testing (Goldacre 2008), believes that trials offer a way to test claims in public policy. He was a co-author of the influential guide to trials published by the Cabinet Office (Haynes et al. 2012). These books show the current importance of rigorous methods in evaluation, and link well to the promotion of behavioural insights which can also be tested by trials.

Psychologists have not been quiet in the rush to the bookshelves and airwaves, not needing the intermediation of the economists. Cialdini has worked on the role of norms in encouraging (or discouraging) pro-social behaviours, for example work on littering, for many years, and his insights have become the common wisdom in this field, such as the experiments that showed that hotel guests were more likely to reuse their towels if told that other guests also did it (Goldstein et al. 2008), and the role of norms in discouraging or encouraging littering (Cialdini et al. 1990). Building on this work, he has written a general book on influence, which again is a book in a trade imprint (Cialdini 2009) and is targeted to a general audience of people seeking to be more effective. Closer to the behavioural agenda is *The Small Big* (Martin et al. 2014), which offers a similar theme to the nudge idea that small things make a difference. This book is linked to a consultancy offering services to the public and private sectors, Influence at Work (see https://www.influenceatwork.com). Dan Ariely has produced a flurry of books which address the behavioural public policy agenda, such as *Irrationally Yours: On Missing Socks, Pickup Lines, and Other Existential Puzzles* (2015).

The profusion of books offering psychological insights into public problems and recommending solutions also gives an impression of the uptake in this agenda. An example is the book *Mindless Eating* (Wansink 2006), which details laboratory research into why people eat indiscriminately and how they are often manipulated into making unwise food choices. Another book, *Reckoning with Risk: Learning to Live with Uncertainty*, examines risk in everyday life, such as how people respond to figures and statistics, and takes forward Kahneman's experiments (Gigerenzer 2003). Another example is Chabris and Simons's (2010) book on intuition and perception, which shows how bias enters into everyday decisions. In the UK, the Royal Society of Arts made a splash on behavioural public policy with its Social Brain project, Transforming Behaviour Change, which takes a broad approach to understanding how cognitions affect behaviour change, deploying research from the neurosciences, as well as more conventional sources in behavioural economics.

What is striking about this review of popular science and commentary is the level of engagement and the sheer range of applications and discussions. Even though these ideas had been developed over a long period of time, there is a sense that from the mid-2000s there had been a change in the intellectual weather that indicated that the time was right for new policy initiatives. Maybe the economic recession that occurred from 2008 caused people to doubt findings from conventional economics and search out new sources of knowledge. As with much diffusion, it is hard to trace the causal processes. It is easier to see connections and detect a trend, but nonetheless it is a plausible line to argue, given the timing and volume of these publications, that these books were responding to a period of intellectual uncertainty.

PUBLIC CRITICISM

Along with the praise comes the criticism, which is mainly reserved for Chapter 6 on the limitations to nudge, and which comes from many quarters. Much is theoretical, such as about the consistency of the term 'libertarian paternalism' or about nudge embodying a neoliberal version of the state in austere times (Leggett 2014). There is also critique from a Foucauldian perspective, such as Whitehead and colleagues, who argue that the use of these techniques strongly impinges on the autonomy of individuals, establishing what they call the 'psychological state' (Jones et al. 2013). The point of raising these criticisms here is not to engage with the attack on the use of behavioural sciences and nudge at this point in the book, but to show how the critiques of nudge are part of the fanning effect behind the phenomenon, reacting to the uptick in interest, in part helping to diffuse it. Controversy can draw attention to a new phenomenon and highlight its importance.

CONCLUSION

The diffusion of ideas about behaviour change, which emerge out of the academy, has been a considerable phenomenon in recent years, coming into prominence over a short space of time. On the surface, this success might seem to be a surprise, given the way in which academic ideas can be difficult to grasp and that policy-makers and commentators find it hard to be interested in theoretical problems. But the diffusion has been easier in this case, partly because the academic advocates themselves were keen to simplify the ideas. Even though there are quite a few technical issues in the literature, at base there is a simple message that many audiences outside economics were willing to hear, which is that the dictates of the rational model need to be modified by a more plausible set of psychological assumptions. As stated in Chapter 3, the actual change in thinking within economics has not been as strong or marked as might be thought. Behavioural economics operates within the mainstream; but the challenge to an orthodoxy is a good message to get across. Critique suggests conflict, which makes for a good story to tell in the media. Advocates write in ways that are easy to understand and consistent with the prior expectations of not only other social scientists but more general readers, who may have always thought the rational model was too demanding but were afraid to challenge it. Thaler (2015), with his talk of 'humans' and 'econs', amplified the tale of rebellion.

The central ideas were synthesised and simplified and made ready for policy-makers in easy-to-understand lists. These acts of translation and simplification became essential in getting a new idea adopted, a conscious process of appealing to the world outside the academy (Flinders 2013). The notion of an idea that catches on is very familiar in studies of

public policy. Critical in this literature is the presence of policy entrepreneurs who can be a useful conduit for ideas (Kingdon 1984). With
talented advocates in the right place and at the right time, ideas for
reforming public policy can become normal and accepted, sometimes
quite quickly. It is a truism in studies of diffusion that innovation takes
the classic S-curve (Rogers 1983), whereby interest can be slow at first,
but then there is a rapid expansion, which can end up as policy. The
pattern appears to fit the expansion of nudge policies. In this process, it is
possible to observe that a certain kind of nudge was appearing, which
was more suited to the policy world. The question to ask is whether the
dynamics of diffusion and translation were encouraging policy-makers to
select certain kinds of nudges, those of a less threatening and uncontro-
versial kind, so they got more acceptability. These choices may have
structured how the research and policy agenda evolved into the nudge
policy agenda of today.

5. Translating nudge into practice: Routes to innovation

At some stage, for all the talk of behavioural insights and studies done in the academy, there is a need to put these ideas into practice. With behavioural public policy, the transfer usually involves an agency or another public body, or sometimes a private company acting in a public way, which can introduce a nudge or behavioural insight into its standard operating procedures. By making a conscious choice to do behavioural public policy, an agency can redesign a policy or procedure that may have existed in the same form for many years, either from past legacies, or from other ideas, or that may even have been adopted unthinkingly. What the use of the behavioural insight involves is a different way of working, a new kind of implementation that has the behavioural insight incorporated as part of the communication or information flow from the organisation. A lot needs to happen, which involves an internal person or unit that wishes to oversee the insight, and then a delivery body, such as an implementation agency, which wishes to carry out the intervention; it requires some interest by a senior person in one of the organisations involved; it then needs authorisation for the intervention taking place, often at a political level; as a result of the authorisation some action has to be decided upon and then followed; then ideally some change takes place as a result of the intervention.

Just as in the world outside behavioural science, inertia and defaults play a role in the implementation of behavioural insights, so the challenge is to find out how to turn the initial enthusiasm for nudge into implemented policies that embody these insights. The question then becomes: what kind of organisational innovation needs to happen so that insights can transfer? In this process, what role do the translators play in disseminating the ideas? Then, within the organisation, are certain officials or individuals important in convincing others to adopt behavioural insights?

In this chapter, the process of organisational translation is investigated to see how innovations happened and what are the mechanisms of diffusion. The idea is to find out why nudge policies emerged when they did and to explain the rapid dissemination and adoption of these ideas in agencies across the world. In addition, it is important to find out whether the tendency toward simplification and the creation of a more practical agenda show the limits to the transfer of nudge and illustrate the pragmatic way in which it has emerged; translation may affect the radicalism of the nudge agenda, which has become associated with providing certain kinds of evidence and the use of robust forms of evaluation that have the power to make findings legitimate and powerful. The topic of experimentation is covered in the next section, before the chapter maps out how the field of behavioural public policy has developed. It is important to understand how experimentation works within an organisation, and how innovations using experimentally tested behavioural public policies intersect with organisational interests and routines. Understanding these processes allows for an assessment of the range of nudge, to find out what it is possible to do in an organisation given current levels of commitment, expertise, and engagement. The discussion also indicates how the use of behavioural insights creates new opportunities for public sector reform.

TESTING AND EXPERIMENTATION

Often involved in the translation into practice is testing – the initial appraisal as to whether an intervention is going to work or not – which becomes part of the initial selling of the idea to the organisation: test, see what works, implement with the successful policy, and then tell others. There are many standard ways of testing policies, such as a desk review of the available evidence, doing a pilot, or carrying out a small study with a few participants or areas. There are better methods of evaluation, whereby what is being tested can be proven to have an effect, usually when compared to a counterfactual or a comparison state of affairs. In terms of translation, the better the test the more stakeholders can be persuaded, as the test has more credibility, though this statement depends on stakeholders believing and understanding the robustness of the method. Sometimes more advanced methods are hard to understand or it is more of a challenge to convey the results simply, whereas low-tech stakeholder assessments and consultancy reports can at times be more effective. The hope is that practitioners understand the robustness of the methods on offer and select the best one for the problem at hand. Some public managers understand the importance of knowing rather than having policies simply legitimated by outside evaluations and consultant reports.

In the world of evaluating policy one method holds sway: this is the randomised controlled trial (RCT) or field experiment (see John 2017a). The RCT relies on randomising participants into an intervention or comparison group and then comparing outcomes afterwards (and if possible before). Randomisation ensures the groups are equivalent and the only thing that distinguishes the groups is the intervention. Comparing the outcomes between the treatment/intervention and control/comparison groups yields the impact of the behavioural cue or other intervention. Researchers and policy-makers can then make a causal inference that the intervention caused the outcomes. RCTs address the main weakness of most methods of evaluation that they cannot separate out the intervention from other factors that affect outcomes (John 2017a). In fact, RCTs are part of a family of methods, such as natural experiments or even quasi-experiments, which make a causal inference by ruling out the influence of observed and unobserved factors that are correlated with the outcome. RCTs have a special place as a method because they are associated with testing an intervention and can mimic whether a policy is introduced or not. Their dominance in medical and health-related evaluations gives them a lot of legitimacy with policy-makers. Most people understand the basic rationale of a trial as having one or more treatment arms and with results generated by comparing outcomes with those in a control group, or comparing outcomes between treatment groups. People know there is a need for a large number of participants and that trials work well in particular situations, such as where there is an opportunity to randomise and outcomes can be measured easily.

RCTs initially got a bad reputation because they were thought hard to carry out in a policy context. This perceived failure was because the early experiments tended to evaluate large-scale social interventions, such as negative income tax, which turned out to be very complex to implement (Ross 1970). These implementation issues meant policy-makers did not get the benefit from trials that they expected, so the method tended to appear in the textbooks and guides (e.g. HM Treasury 2011) but was not often used in practice, except in the work and welfare domain, whose researchers overcame the problems of the early social interventions (Gueron and Rolston 2013). This relative fall from fashion in the 1970s and 1980s has been countered by a recent interest from scholars across social science disciplines, in particular economics (List 2011) and political science (Green and Gerber 2003). Social scientists rediscovered the usefulness of trials and discovered contexts where they could be implemented effectively and yield cumulative advantages, such as Get Out the Vote (GOTV) experiments, which can evaluate what kind of intervention causes voters to turn out at the polls (Green and Gerber

2015). It soon became normal for behavioural economists to use experiments to test out behavioural theories (as highlighted in Chapter 3), which of course links to the frequent use of trials in psychology. Moreover, they can test out causal mechanisms, especially if there are multiple treatment arms. Once the idea got raised that agencies can do the experiments themselves, RCTs did not seem so radical, especially when behavioural economists and others got involved in partnerships with agencies to deliver these experiments.

Behavioural interventions work very well when tested with trials. The key advantage is that prior research produces a number of recommendations that can be applied to relatively discrete stages of the delivery process. Consider, for example, a favourite of behavioural interventions, which is the redesign of a letter encouraging someone to settle up a payment, which has been used by HM Revenue and Customs (HMRC), the UK tax collection agency, to encourage people to pay their debts at an earlier date (Hallsworth et al. 2017). The discretion of the policy-maker is in the wording of these letters and whether different phrases can be included alongside the normal and standard reminder text. The wording can be changed without recourse to legal advice. It is possible to give the instructions to send the different letters, then to examine the payment accounts of those who have been written to, and to tie the payment outcomes with the identifiers that say which treatment group they are in. It is then possible to produce tables of payment rates and the treatment allocation, and run standard tests of statistical significance between the average of payments or proportions in each group. The key is to design the different wordings so there is a comparison of feasible alternatives. As discussed earlier, these trials do not provide a pure test of a psychological mechanism that would always stand peer review in a psychological science journal which would be better delivered in a laboratory setting; they are simply tests that assess what it is practical for government to do in particular situations. Often the trial arms are decided in an interaction between the client and the researcher, with each bouncing ideas back and forth. The idea is not to test a theory, but to find something that works. At all times the agency is very much in charge, and the science has to fit within political and organisational constraints.

The Behavioural Insights Team (BIT), discussed in more detail below, has made great play with trials, though it took about 18 months to get them fully established into its work programme. Trials were championed by the publication *Test, Learn, Adapt: Developing Public Policy with Randomised Controlled Trials* (Haynes et al. 2012). The taxes and fines reminder studies were done as trials (Behavioural Insights Team 2012), as was early work on charitable giving (Cabinet Office and Charitable

Aid Foundation 2013). Trials quickly became the signature of the unit, and developed in scale and ambition over time, such as the trial of welfare-to-work at Loughton, Essex, which was turned into a stepped-wedge (staged) trial throughout the whole county (see Halpern 2015). The use of trials continued when the team was spun out of government and characterises its work on standards and attainment in education, for example (see Behavioural Insights Team 2015). The team was keen to do trials where they were relatively easy to do, that is when there were clear and numerous units to randomise, as with tax reminders, and when the agency was already collecting outcome data, so not placing huge burdens on the agency, making the experience not too onerous but impactful in terms of results that could be useful. Many of the early trials of the team yielded large financial savings. With some extrapolation, which makes use of assumptions, such as the effect of the trial being long lasting and the results externally valid across a large UK or England population, it is possible to come up with annual savings of many millions of pounds that can be claimed by BIT as a benefit for the agency and a fulfilment of the objectives of its political principals.

The demonstration work of the team probably encouraged a more general use of trials throughout UK government, where they have become a more normal practice. One example is a large-scale trial carried out by the former Department for Business, Innovation and Skills, testing whether getting online advice for business support and a growth voucher would be good for businesses (Department for Business, Innovation and Skills and Cabinet Office 2014), which was designed by BIT. Such use of trials has been encouraged by their rapid adoption in the United States, in particular for education, work mirrored in the interventions commissioned in the UK by the Education Endowment Foundation and other initiatives, such as the London Schools Excellence Fund, which has worked with the evaluation champion Project Oracle and its partnership organisation, The Social Innovation Partnership (TSIP). At the same time, the government set up What Works research and evidence centres where strong forms of evaluation, such as randomised controlled trials, are privileged. It can be seen that a variety of influences going beyond behavioural interventions have promoted the use of trials in government and by other agencies. The level of experience of running them has been growing strongly over time. It makes this kind of testing of programmes more feasible and gives a more scientific underpinning to evaluation. This is probably as significant a development in public policy as the use of behavioural sciences, and again the expertise has come from economics, while academic psychology does not feature very much, with other disciplines, such as education and crime science, also contributing.

In fact, there is a huge diversity in the kind of work being carried out. It is possible then to see that part of the reason for the fast diffusion of behavioural insights is that they were tested with pragmatic and relatively easy-to-do trials, which yielded savings, and that the details were released to the media.

EARLY USES OF BEHAVIOURAL INSIGHTS IN BRITAIN

As was discussed in Chapter 3, policy-makers in Britain took an interest in the behavioural agenda right from the early days (see John and Richardson 2012). In the UK, central government departments found out about it by commissioning reports from their research staff. One of the leading departments, before the reform of the structure of government in 2016, was the Department for Environment, Food and Rural Affairs (Defra), which had been pioneering policies for climate change, such as energy consumption and encouraging people to buy and use more energy-efficient appliances. The department had a long history of research into this area, and had been using behaviour change as a core part of its mission, influencing the design of regulation as well as nudges. It published a report, *A Framework for Pro-environmental Behaviours*, in 2008 (Defra 2008). The department had been increasingly aware of the importance of seeking to change citizen behaviour in order to reach policy goals, carrying out a series of internal reviews (e.g. Pike et al. 2010). HMRC also developed an early interest in behaviour modification in relation to tax payments, and carried out pioneering experiments into changing information about reminders for tax returns, consulting with Steve Martin, one of Cialdini's colleagues. The Department of Health has a long tradition of research into health behaviours, so ironically is less part of the wave of enthusiasm for nudge, having its own long-running research and policy agenda. In a supplementary memorandum to the House of Lords enquiry by the Department of Health (BC 151), the department reported on the extensive amount of research it carries out that has important elements on behaviour change. It helped set up a Policy Research Unit on Behaviour and Health, located at the University of Cambridge (see http://www.bhru.iph.cam.ac.uk/about-us/).

There were other routes for the influence of behavioural economics and other research to enter into government policy, such as the role of the Government Economics Service, which also produced guidance in 2008 about how behavioural economics could be used to inform policy (John and Richardson 2012). The Government Social Research Service was another generic source of information (as was the Central Office of Information); the Government Statistical Service and numerous advisory bodies also play a role. Potential coordination was increased because Government Economic and Social Research (GESR) was created from merging the Government Economics Service and the Government Social Research Service. There was increasing coordination across government, as evidenced by the appointment of Rachel McCloy, a psychologist from the University of Reading, in a Public Sector Placement Fellowship. With these precursors, the Behavioural Insights Team built on existing good practice in central government.

In a survey of the use of behavioural insights in 2012, a report concluded that, 'In spite of the large amount of social science advice that government receives overall, it is hard to resist the conclusion that the overall provision for behaviour change at the moment tends to be patchy, dependent on departmental initiatives and ministerial interest' (John and Richardson 2012: 20). The Green Alliance in its submission to the House of Lords' behaviour change inquiry captures the criticism very well: 'We are starting to see movement in the right direction with behavioural units being set up in DECC, CLG and DfT, and pockets of people in the Cabinet Office. Yet these posts are not yet core to the policy creation process, and the rational actor model is still largely prevailing' (House of Lords 2011). These views were iterated by the House of Lords Select Committee on Behaviour Change, which thought that the focus on non-compulsory or non-regulatory policies risked neglecting the more powerful interventions that government knows work. Though there was a lack of applied research on changing behaviour at a population level, there is other available evidence that the government needs to use to better effect. The House of Lords' review of behaviour change policies found that, although it received some examples of evidence-based policies, such as policies on energy-efficient products and smoking cessation services, there were many examples of policies that had not taken account of available evidence, including policies on food labelling and alcohol pricing (House of Lords 2011: 5). The question to ask is whether, over six years after the publication of the report, the policy agenda has moved on.

As with central government there has been a long tradition of seeking to promote behaviour change in local government, but confined to particular areas such as transport and the environment, often occurring in the larger strategic councils, such as the county and metropolitan authorities. The growth of interest in behavioural economics was confined to a few pioneering councils, often because chief executives, other officers or politicians got interested in the idea. The way the process works is through active local authorities examining the whole of their policy machinery and finding out where to input behaviour change ideas. For example, in December 2010 West Sussex had a challenge session where it set out the principles of behaviour change, inviting representatives from departments. Other councils have had initiatives more focused on individual services, such as work by Coventry City Council and iMPOWER, and also Croydon. Other examples are the London Borough of Sutton, which sought to remodel its transport service, and the London Borough of Barnet, with its policies on green champions. Kent has extensive policies, such as employing a behaviour change manager. Salford has been pioneering work on health. Many of these nudge-based policies pre-dated the Coalition Government (2010–2015) and even the publication of *Nudge* (Thaler and Sunstein 2008). Such examples of good practice were diffused in existing networks of good practice sponsored by the Local Government Association, such as its communities of practice (CoPs).

THE BEHAVIOURAL INSIGHTS TEAM

The setting up of the Behavioural Insights Team, a unit in the Cabinet Office working directly to the prime minister, in the summer of 2010 is a story that has been well told (e.g. John 2014), in particular by its director, David Halpern, in his book *Inside the Nudge Unit* (2015). It is a tale of small beginnings and the way in which the unit built on the gradual diffusion of ideas about behavioural sciences described above. It benefited from the backing of the Conservative leader David Cameron and his advisors, who were interested in behaviour change and social policy, and what could be done to create a more pro-social citizenry, a project called the Big Society. Gus O'Donnell was still in place as head of the civil service and was ready to propose the idea to the incoming government, and of course it had as its director the same David Halpern who had played such a critical role in generating enthusiasm for behavioural ideas when he was in the Strategy Unit in the previous Labour Government.

It started with just seven members, taking up just about half of a long, shared desk in the cavernous offices at 1 Whitehall. Most were career civil servants seconded from other units, with only Halpern as a psychologist, later joined by Laura Haynes. Paul Dolan, a behavioural economist, was a team member for a short period of time. The team could not be called a psychological unit, as its approach was more practical, keen on building relationships around Whitehall and its environs and getting a sense of excitement going. Although it was plugged into the academic community, with the Academic Advisory Panel set up in 2011,[1] the approach was to take some appealing ideas and apply them to practical problems of government departments and other agencies. A long cast list of celebrity academics, such as the psychologist Dan Ariely, came through Whitehall to give talks and attend meetings, and they also provided proposals to test. Team members gave presentations to government departments around Whitehall and had many meetings with officials to discuss how behavioural ideas could be applied to policies being developed. From these interactions, some officials came forward with proposals for behavioural interventions that were developed in partnership with members of the team. The team was in effect providing a service to these departments, which was free at first. Team members also did desk research of different options as studied in the literature to identify ones to test.

The approach was to convey behavioural ideas as clearly as possible. This was symbolised by the simplification of the MINDSPACE acronym (Hallsworth et al. 2010), with its basis in the economics and psychology literatures, to the shorter and more straightforward EAST (easy, attractive, social and, timely) (Service et al. 2014). In presentations and their publications, the team stressed the straightforward nature of their interventions and how big problems often have simple solutions. For example, over measures to encourage households to install energy-saving devices in their homes, team members emphasised that the main reason for lack of adoption of insulation was that people did not want to clear their lofts, and uptake increased fourfold when households were offered free loft clearance (Department of Energy and Climate Change 2013). When presented with a slide showing a cluttered loft, audience members could not help smiling as they saw their weak selves in the example. The result is that officials in Whitehall and elsewhere felt they owned such unthreatening findings and research, and wished to apply these new ideas in their own departments or agencies.

The team was very public about its work, and there is no sense of it being a secret cabal unleashing a programme of control of citizens around Whitehall (see John 2017b). It was interested in trail-blazing the proof of the concepts. This was very much true of the work on speeding up debt recovery using behavioural insights, summarised in the document *Fraud, Error and Debt: Behavioural Insights Team Paper* (Behavioural Insights Team 2012). The document is a guide to the work that has been done, containing studies by the team as well as summaries from desk reviews. It very much spoke to the agenda of government departments, seeking to add value on the top of policies that had already been agreed. The changes it encouraged were not radical step-shifts in citizen compliance with government ideas and policies, but modest changes based on

working along the grain of citizen preferences. Many behavioural interventions, although having their origins in academic work, were easily
comprehensible, such as personalising SMS text messages to encourage
citizens to pay their court fines (Haynes et al. 2013). This use of nudge is
consistent with a more citizen-friendly form of governance whereby
innovations are adopted that take the viewpoint of hard-pressed citizens
seeking to manage their lives. Nudge needs bureaucrats who understand
how people think rather than those who roll out interventions designed in
a psychological lab (John et al. 2011).

Like any small unit operating in the relatively decentralised context of
British government, where the centre does not have absolute power and
itself resembles a feudal court rather than a commander and enforcer (see
Burch and Holliday 1996), the team needed to persuade other parts of
government to take part and then share in the glory. It worked in a
competitive environment of credit-claiming and searches for ministerial
attention, but it survived relatively unscathed in spite of the inevitable
spats and turf wars. It may have benefited from a shift in focus from the
centre of government toward a concern with delivery and implementation, which had happened under prime ministers Blair and Brown. The
1997–2010 Labour Government's focus on delivery was epitomised by
the employment of the arch-moderniser Michael Barber. The implementation focus carried on under the Coalition Government (2010–2015),
especially as it was hard to agree major policy objectives between the
two political parties.

BIT achieved a positive impact in the media, getting a good press from
both left-of-centre publications (e.g. Benjamin 2013) and the right-wing
press (e.g. Bell 2013). What many of these write-ups on the unit show is
that journalists started out with a story about manipulation and the role of
psychologists using their expertise to trick the citizens. In the end, they
were won over by the common-sense approach and added value of such
techniques. There was a similar kind of reaction in the public commentary and assessment of nudge policies. Initially there was some resistance
to the use of nudge policies and the role of the BIT, with the argument
that such an approach was designed to prevent the use of the strong tools
of government. Critics believed nudge was a covert way of justifying a
retreat of the state, and entrenched the role of the private sector in
government in fields such as food labelling (House of Lords 2011).
Academics have made the same kind of argument: nudge was not strong
enough to achieve effective behaviour change and a more robust
approach would be better (Marteau et al. 2011). However, few critics
directly criticised nudge-based initiatives. Behaviour change advocates
have instead criticised the idea that nudge implies that behavioural

interventions apply just to information campaigns and the manipulation of defaults, whereas in fact behavioural science can be applied more generally across the tools of government to inform how they work (see Oliver 2013b).

In short, the team was a success and has been adroit in managing its external reputation. Its good fortune depended on responding to the political agenda, and working with government departments and agencies. It mainly tweaked existing policies and implementation procedures rather than imposed an integrated vision. Above all, it carried out its tasks in a way that was public and transparent. Its record seems a long way from the image of the psychological state (Jones et al. 2013), and more about the way in which a relatively small team was able to craft useful improvements to standard procedures and help public officials get better traction on how policies are implemented (John 2017b). The team publicised its policies to encourage more debate and take-up of behavioural insights.

BEHAVIOURAL INSIGHTS, RCTS AND INNOVATION

Work in organisational theory examines the conditions that can help organisations become more innovative. In the private sector, such innovation is associated with new products and higher profitability (Argyris 1993; Nooteboom 2000), but in the public sector it is often about policy changes and better approaches to public sector management (Kelman 2005; NAO 2009). Writers in this literature outline the forces for conservatism within organisations, which are due to the power of routines, psychological factors and standard operating procedures, which tend to benefit those in power. Existing power-holders may resist new policies because they are associated with younger post-holders whose careers might benefit. Against this can be arrayed forces for innovation that can overcome such resistance, whose advocates are often concentrated in small groups in the organisation's bureaucracy. But these reform groups need nurturing and must build a successful coalition to overcome change. In addition, there is a long-held assumption that innovation is hard to achieve in the public sector because of the lack of the profit motive. Moreover, lines of accountability to political office-holders mean that bureaucrats have limited discretion to innovate independently. Nonetheless, in the right conditions innovation can occur (Borins 2002), and it is possible to read across the private and public sectors, taking note of the context of each when assessing what factors drive innovation.

BIT has all the hallmarks of an innovator: it promoted new ideas and ways of working, and it has been successful in promoting innovation (see John 2013b, 2014). The literature on organisational change provides a good description of how the unit was set up and operated, and how senior sponsorship allowed it to do new things and operate in part against the grain. One assumes that the politicians and civil servants knew what they were doing when they hired Halpern to direct the unit, as he had performed a similar role with the Labour Government. The Cabinet Secretary must have expected that the unit would attempt to foster innovation, and this fitted with his outlook as an unconventional civil servant. The retirement of O'Donnell did not affect the success and legitimacy of the unit. Halpern and his unit were able to deliver to the prime minister successes in an otherwise bleak environment for the government. The costs of operating the unit were low, and there were few risks, especially since journalists liked it too. One can imagine why the politicians were happy to sponsor it and that other parts of government were content to follow this central lead.

It shows what can be done with a modest level of investment by the centre. Whether such units are time limited is beyond the scope of this book (and it may be the case that BIT got out at the right time – see below), and it is clear that bureaucratic routines and the demands of governing take priority in the long term. But when there is the right balance of environment, structures, and people it is possible to produce more innovation at the centre of British government, and similar stories can be told for other countries and locales. The key is relative openness in a complex institutional structure and a willingness to work across boundaries.

FROM SPECIAL UNIT TO INTERNATIONAL NOT-FOR-PROFIT

In the end, the directors of BIT realised this particular model of innovation as a unit within the bureaucracy could not be sustained indefinitely. Unlike a company that needs a unit to ensure product development over many decades, the tendency for units to follow fashion is more the case in the febrile world of central government. In fact, the surprise about BIT was that it had lasted so long, and that it had been able to network and build political support rather than having automatic protection from a few senior people, especially when the unit grew in size over time. David Halpern and members of the team still work closely with senior officials at the permanent secretary level, and also network across government and agencies, such as by running seminars and the training events for civil servants, the policy schools.

In government, BIT found itself constrained by rules and regulations which made it hard to carry out behavioural interventions, even purchasing the materials to carry out trials, and to engage other experts, to bid for funds, or to massively expand staff at the same time as the civil service wanted to reduce numbers of employees. In 2014, it ran a bidding round for outsiders to own the organisation along with government so that it could carry out its central government work on a framework contract. On receiving bids, the government invited Nesta, the organisation that has an endowment from the National Lottery and works on projects for the public good, to be the partner, so that the current owners of the unit are the government, Nesta, and the employees.

When BIT moved out of government, staff numbers expanded dramatically, and it opened new offices in New York, Singapore, and Manchester (UK). It had previously had a staff member working in Sydney for the New South Wales Government, in the unit Behavioural Insights, and it has expanded its operation in Australia. Numbers of staff increased to nearly 90 in the London office alone, and the range of projects increased to include international work on behavioural insights, such as in development and corruption. This growth reflects the diffusion of behavioural insights and BIT's success in promoting this agenda. Many of the insights were still quite conventional, but the range of applications was increasing. BIT was careful to avoid being like an international consultancy, keeping its academic contacts and research agenda, and also getting funding from foundations rather than just from private or governmental sources. The charge of following private interests through what appears to be privatisation of a government asset can be refuted by reference to the government, Nesta, and its own employees having shares, with the first two firmly as public service organisations and key to the governance of BIT. It is important to counter appearances. Moreover, much of the dynamism remains intact even though the unit progressed from using insights in an accessible and easy way. BIT has played a role in the international diffusion of behavioural insights as used by government and agencies across the world, through its extensive network of international contacts and where other governments have seen BIT as a model to emulate. Although the team employs social psychologists, the modal background is economics, and Michael Sanders, director of research (chief scientific officer) at the team, is a behavioural economist.

Meanwhile, the behavioural agenda continues in government with the formation of a behavioural economics unit within HMRC, Behaviour

Change Knowledge Network, with good links across government. Behavioural ideas diffuse to other jurisdictions, such as to local government, with local councils redesigning the considerable amounts of information and regulations they convey to citizens, such as local tax reminders (see Blume and John 2014), or encouraging a channel shift to the online delivery of services (John and Blume 2017). The behavioural agenda works well in a decentralised arena where agencies focus on delivery and relationships with customers and citizens. Agencies can try out different ideas and customise their messages and regulations in different contexts.

TRANSLATION TO OTHER CONTEXTS

From their origins in the UK and USA, behavioural insights have been translated into practice in a large number of jurisdictions, where they reflect the developments highlighted in previous chapters, and are based on a diffusion of the success of behavioural insights as pioneered by BIT. One survey found 51 countries that have central state-led policy initiatives (Whitehead et al. 2014: 7). The number has probably gone up considerably since 2014. The survey found that non-government organisations were important in disseminating these ideas, which relate to the policy diffusion literature that focuses on intermediators and translators (Graham et al. 2013). In addition, 136 states out of 196 had initiatives that were influenced by the behavioural sciences. International organisations have been very influential, as the World Bank's (2015) *World Development Report* indicates, but it appears that behavioural insights have been thought to be essential in testing out aid and development policies, especially as trials are a very important tool of evaluation in this field. Overall, the view of many commentators is that nudge has gone beyond fashion and faddishness and has become embedded as a standard practice in public policy. In 2017, the Organisation for Economic Co-operation and Development (OECD) produced an enumeration of case studies of behavioural public policy, which came from across the world; its foreword states: 'The report finds that the use of behavioural insights has moved beyond a trend' (OECD 2017: 3).

Nudge units have become important elsewhere. In the USA, where it is to be expected that behavioural ideas would be influential, the political context can also be critical of social sciences. The long-running anti-intellectualism of US life and suspicion of the elites of the East coast go back to the populist movements of the 1890s, anti-Communism in the 1950s, George Wallace's presidential campaign, the Reagan revolution, and extend to the election of Trump to the presidency in 2016. The vast investment in social and behavioural science is countered by this negative political culture and its effect on policy-makers. Nevertheless, behavioural initiatives found favour under President Obama, first with Cass Sunstein's appointment as head of the Office of Information and Regulatory Affairs, though much of this role was about simplification of administrative procedures rather than the full application of behavioural insights (see Sunstein 2014b). A more recent initiative was the Social and Behavioral Sciences Team (CBST), which was organised under the remit of the National Science and Technology Council, receiving support from the Office of Evaluation Sciences and the General Services Administration. It implemented Executive Order 13707, 'Using behavioral science insights to better serve the American people'. As with BIT, there were message-based interventions, such as a newly designed letter that increased farmers' access to credit, messages to low-income families, and a single email that went to service members that doubled the rate of involvement for a savings plan, followed by face-to-face meetings to fill out a form requiring a forced choice (Dubner 2016). The unit had projects that ranged from increasing the efficiency of the bureaucracy to dealing with responses to climate change. Predictably, President Trump did not support the unit, and its staff were dispersed to other agencies on 21 January 2017.

These changes in organisational priorities in the UK, USA and elsewhere highlight the importance of the political sanction of nudge, as it depends on political principals who are sympathetic, such as Cameron and his Cabinet ministers in the UK case, and Obama in the USA. A change of leader can alter all that, such as in the UK in 2016, where the new prime minister, Theresa May, was less interested in nudge. In part, that is because the UK government was facing the bigger problem of delivering Brexit. It also reflected May's brand of Conservativism, which meant she was less interested in following modern trends than Cameron (though she was part of the reform of the Conservative Party, and her phrase 'the nasty party' was an injunction to modernise). Under her leadership, the Home Office was more resistant to using behavioural insights than other government departments. Such changes show the limits to the diffusion of nudge as well as the opportunities. Prime ministers come and go. At the time of writing, May's future is less secure, since the Conservative Party lost seats and became a minority government after the 2017 General Election.

The contingent nature of the diffusion in the US and UK is replicated elsewhere, and the adoption of nudge reflects the local circumstances. In the Netherlands, there has been considerable interest, but the adoption of behaviour, insights into policy reflects departmental strengths and there is no central nudge unit as a result. The use of behavioural science in the Netherlands – as elsewhere – is dispersed, which reflects different understandings of the research programme as well as institutional fragmentation (Feitsma and Schillemans 2016). There is a unit operating in the German federal government. In some places nudge units do not find favour, such as with the Australian federal government: proposals were put to the incoming Liberal administration in 2013 (John 2013c), but the government did not at first set up a nudge unit or the equivalent. Then there was a change of heart and the Behavioural Economics Team of the Australian Government (BETA) was set up, starting its work in February 2016. In France, the employment of Olivier Oullier in the Centre for Strategic Analysis of the Prime Minister seemed to indicate the value of a cognitive behavioural scientist at the centre of government. But nudge ideas were ridiculed in the French press, and the subsequent administration under President Hollande did not go down the behavioural policy route. French intellectuals and commentators were more critical of what are thought to be American or Anglo-Saxon imports that smack of neoliberalism (even though there is no bias toward competition and the small state in nudge). Consistent with the story told in Chapter 4 and above, there is a varied response to behavioural insights from organisations, with resistance to the new ideas as well as enthusiasm for them. The OECD report notes 'a concern among practitioners that knowledge transfer will not happen. Networks of practitioners have experienced a certain resistance from some of their members in sharing the results of their work' (OECD 2017: 19).

Diffusion has gone upwards and downwards. It has gone upwards to international organisations, such as the World Bank, where behavioural insights have started to be applied to international aid programmes to improve their effectiveness. The OECD published a report on behavioural economics (Lunn 2014). It set up a network to promote its ideas, The European Nudging Network (TEN), managed by the Initiative for Science, Society and Policy (ISSP) in collaboration with the OECD and HEC Paris; it was created in 2014 to disseminate applied behavioural insights in Europe and elsewhere. It held a seminar, Behavioural Insights and New Approaches to Policy Design, on 23 January 2015, with people attending from central and local governments, regulators, staff of international organisations, and academics. Another recipient of behavioural ideas is the European Commission, which also produced a report (Sousa et al. 2016) and where the Joint Research Centre (JRC) offers support to other Commission services by providing behavioural insights. The OECD produced its own report (OECD 2017) with the idea of disseminating good practice. Private consultancies have also assisted the diffusion, as part of their work is enthusing and communicating as well as being commissioned to do evaluations. An example is Ideas42 (discussed in Chapter 4). Output from the journals of the professional associations, such as the Behavioral Science and Policy Association (BSPA), is intended to be read by practitioners, diffusing ideas in blogs and tweets linked to research articles and shorter pieces.

Local authorities have been in the vanguard though have been less celebrated. Given the multiplicity of local authorities, there are bound to be some innovators even if the rest are laggards. Policy often diffuses through the local level by imitation and emulation (see Ward and John 2013). As already noted for the UK, much of the earlier innovation happened at the local level. It is often regional and local governments that are very interested in behavioural innovation.

Behavioural policy has diffused in ways that depend on the context and willingness to deploy these ideas. Nudge needs to be seen as feasible and acceptable by the elected politicians and elites in a society or else it is not going to work or be adopted. It needs champions to push it forward as a project that has to have publicity and good reception to behavioural initiatives. In this way, the progress of behavioural ideas is political in the wider sense of that term, in that ideas need to work alongside political interests, and nudge advocates need to respond to the agenda of existing power-holders. Nudge then has not been used to transform the state, such as by being a new set of ideas that can be used by authoritarian politicians seeking greater control and compliance over the citizens (though it can be used in this way, such as for combating terrorism or discouraging migration); rather it usually works within the fragmented and complex structure of government and agencies, and where advocates are seeking to advance new ideas. It is important to get the attention of senior policy-makers and those responsible for the delivery of policies. Nudge has been successful because it has worked within the existing agenda of public policies and according to the standard operating procedures of the bureaucracies. It appeals to the prior aims of bureaucrats and to those wanting more efficiency and traction from public policies rather than system-changers or people seeking uniform controls over citizens.

CONCLUSION

How far to nudge is a product of what is possible politically and organisationally. As nudges need sanction from real-world institutions, such ideas are constrained and structured by who uses them as well as who promotes them. A research agenda needs successes; it has to work for politicians and bureaucrats in terms of responding to and solving current policy problems. In previous chapters, it was shown how the behavioural agenda expanded outward from some narrow theoretical debates to more practical concerns. In this chapter, the next step has been taken, and it is shown how an agenda is helped by advocacy within public organisations, and the impact of implementing such policies that appeal to politicians and bureaucrats located in agencies. It is no surprise that nudges based on simplification work well. It is a relatively small number of nudges that work most often, such as norms (though this may be a product of the nudges that have been tried rather than a full record of what is possible from the population of possible nudges). There is a focus on high-volume financial transactions, where it is relatively easy to modify communication flows. Cases where the architecture shifts, such as with Driver and Vehicle Licensing Agency (DVLA) experiments on organ donation, are rare, and the vast bulk of behavioural insights build on various kinds of enhanced messaging.

It is no surprise that such specialist units work in this practical way and seek to adapt to existing policies and routines. For example, feminist think tanks of the 1980s in the end had to operate in the mainstream, but this compromise may have diluted their radicalism (Eisenstein 1991). Even with this constraint, a special unit in the bureaucracy can promote innovation, which happened with BIT, especially in the early days when it made advances across Whitehall. The unit worked collaboratively across government, translated ideas, and ensured that they were regarded as pragmatic. The work of the unit as an internal propagator of ideas was enhanced by its role in translating ideas internationally, making the later expansion of the unit an extension of this role.

These feedback effects continue to the time of writing in 2017, often from the actions of advocates and nudge units promoting behavioural insights that work. They attract attention, which legitimates the ideas, gets other agencies interested, and so sustains the agenda. The question arises as to whether this attention to behavioural insights is going to continue and whether the agenda can deliver a more radical set of reforms. To what extent are only positive findings reported, limiting the extent of knowledge acquisition? That nudge policies are contingent on the context makes them depend on pre-existing alliances and interests. When those interests change, so does the research and policy agenda. To anticipate the potential for a backlash, the alleged limitations of nudge are considered in the next chapter.

NOTE

1. The author is a member of the panel.

6. Is nudge all it's cracked up to be? Limitations and criticisms

In assessing how far to nudge, it is important to acknowledge possible criticisms of this kind of intervention, in particular of the power and range of its effects. As has been pointed out in the earlier chapters, there is a considerable momentum behind the agenda of behaviour change, and a large number of positive findings have been produced from evaluations and academic studies, which give an impression that everything nudge-like works and that public services are being transformed as a result. To move forward, is it simply a case of expanding the remit of behavioural insights to include more agencies and more contexts, harvesting the gains, and rolling out the reformed procedures and policies? Naturally, no policy and research agenda is going to be transformative in quite such a way, no matter what benefits there are. Thus, this chapter is the place for talking more cautiously about the agenda of nudge, not to knock it down, but to understand some of its limitations and come to a more balanced assessment of how far to nudge. To this end, some of the conventional criticisms of nudge are reviewed, and the chapter also assesses the more damning attacks that have been mounted.

LIMITED RANGE

The first criticism of nudge is that the range of nudges is limited because they tend to focus on a limited subset of activities for which messages can be delivered. Nudges work well for messages, texts, and other forms of communication, which can be directed to the people who get them and are easy to receive and read. They work well when there is a clear interest for people in complying with the prompt or responding to the cue. In other cases, they may be well disposed to do the act if it is in accordance with their values, such as when deciding to donate their organs for use after their death. They may do something when prompted to do so or, in the Thaler and Sunstein (2008) version of behaviour change, respond to a default option that corresponds to their underlying preferences. But in spite of the massive expansion of these kinds of nudges in many contexts, ranging from local to international, it is easy to see that there may be a limited range for these kinds of interventions. Although there are a lot of communications from government, there are limits to the numbers of letters, emails, and texts that can be sent. Though this limit to the capacity to use nudge may vary across governments, with HMRC, for example, sending many millions of letters each year, many agencies use fewer communications. For example, a defence agency might be interested in recruitment, so might want to send messages to get a better representation in its employees, and there might be many internal messages that need to be conveyed. But in practice defence is about maintaining security: conducting operations and getting the logistical back-up in place for them. If managing these operational matters is what a defence facility is all about, how far can behavioural insights be applied in this sector? Behavioural insights might be out of range for some government activities.

The other issue is whether there are enough defaults to generate pro-social outcomes by status quo bias. A default relies on there being a status quo option of complying with a pro-social or beneficial action, but there are many areas where none exists, or where default is the non-beneficial do-nothing decision, such as not applying to university. It is not possible to design a default of attending university, say through an automatic application: the student has to choose actively this option. It is of course possible to design websites with defaults in them, and pension schemes can offer this, but it is easy to see that such a range of these kinds of offers can be limited and that default options cannot be standardised across all government services. In the end, defaults are going to be useful but they are hardly a panacea to improve public policy outcomes.

In other cases, individuals might not be willing to be well disposed to doing the action, who may be hard to influence, making the nudge difficult to apply for these people. With actions that involve entrenched behaviours, such as in health and crime, where people like doing the behaviours and also get benefits from them, light-touch nudges are not going to work well. There are a number of eminent academics and practitioners who make the argument that these limitations are critical for nudge. Marteau et al. (2011) are prominent in this debate, as they suggest that nudge does not address fundamental issues in behaviour change.

In answer to these questions, it is possible to return to the core claims set out at the start of this book, which are about the link between the tools of government and the behavioural public policy reform agenda. Behavioural public policy can reshape the information environment of public policy, which requires the simultaneous implementation of steps in a causal chain, where there are a variety of instruments to be deployed, which range across laws, commands, incentives, organisational levels, and networks. The tools can operate in a customary manner, with the key decision being about their authorisation. But with behavioural insights, it is possible to redesign them so they function much better, whether operating outside the organisation on citizens or other organisations, or inside the organisation for its operating procedures and internal communications. The approach to bias and the discovery of more powerful mechanisms apply to the implementation chain just as much as to the classic soft forms of communication like letters. The task then becomes to identify the links, to find out the key joins and implementation gaps, and then to devise behavioural measures to improve the working of each part. By identifying and meeting these gaps, positive feedback may be unleashed in the organisation, so increasing overall performance, often by more than the sum of the impacts of each link in the chain.

A good example of this approach to applying behavioural insights is the Behavioural Insights Team (BIT) study with the UK Department for Work and Pensions of the employment service at Loughton (see Behavioural Insights Team 2015). The team was charged with reforming searching for work in the organisation and sought to look at all the activities that claimants were obliged to do and how effective were the organisational procedures, such as the number of signatures that were needed to complete the applications. Through the use of behavioural knowledge, it was possible to reform the procedures in the light of the experience of the individual and the cognitive burdens imposed. It was also possible to insert other behavioural measures, such as asking claimants to set out a plan using behavioural science to increase motivations, using the work of Gollwitzer (1999) on 'implementation intentions'. As a result of these innovations, the whole organisation can work better, as was the case in Loughton, for example with a 5 per cent increase in people moving off benefits, which was replicated (with lower effects) in a stepped-wedge trial, where the implementation was done across the county in random (or near-random) order of job centres. In this context, it is also possible to show that behavioural interventions work with groups beyond the normal citizens well disposed toward carrying out tasks and apply to a wider range of actions, and within the complex implementation chains of a bureaucracy. Thinking about the defence example just mentioned, it is possible for responsiveness and efficiency to be improved from the use of behavioural insights through thinking through links in an implementation chain, which might even end up on the battlefield!

New generations of experimenters are increasing the range of interventions and their traction, for example by looking at persuasion effects, which deploy stronger techniques to shift attitudes and behaviours. The reason these experiments are interesting is that for many years it has been assumed they need to go with the grain of people's expectations, which explains the apparently limited range of experiments. But this research shows it is possible to customise interventions that move people from their settled preferences. Broockman and Kalla (2016) find that using transgender canvassers reduces prejudice, even as the result of a ten-minute conversation. This intervention is not a classic behaviour change cue, but it might be expected that it could lead to changes in behaviours in due course, such as voting, even where people do not agree in the first place with the proposition.

WEAK EFFECTS

The second main criticism of nudge is that its interventions do not deliver strong effects or have such small effects they are not worth doing when compared to other options. Overall, they do not offer much of a panacea in spite of the trumpeted claims for benefits. Although a lot of attention is given to nudge policies, when they are examined they tend to have effect sizes that are small percentage point differences, which can appear large when presented in attractive bar charts compared to a control arm, but in fact do not deliver as much uplift as many common interventions already do. The criticism is that this is precisely because they are nudges, that they do not have much power to change behaviour and are really gentle interventions. They are not able to address fundamental social problems that have embedded causes. Moreover, behaviour change theories focus on individual-level rather than societal change (Jones et al. 2013: 51).

It is true that many behavioural insights give percentage uplifts of less than 10 per cent; however, in the light of their cheapness, and because many other factors determine the outcomes concerned, these changes are significant, especially given the light-touch nature of the interventions. It is a question of perception. If the interventions are seen as part of a general movement to activate citizens, then these effects may cumulate over time. When done in an organisational context it is possible for these influences to sum together and feed off each other.

The other issue is to question whether they are weak effects in any case. While many interventions have small effect sizes, others are large. Even Marteau et al. (2011: 264), critics of nudge, report that placing fruit by the cash register increases the amount of fruit bought by school children at lunchtime by 70 per cent (Just and Wansink 2009). The example shows how very simple interventions can lead to large changes in behaviour across a whole range of activities, which is a simple example of changing choice architectures. The weak treatment argument also misses the fundamental point about nudge policies, which is that they achieve strength from the precision of their psychological effects. The argument is that 'small is big' when interventions are attuned to people's perceptions and cognitions. Small changes in communication can have beneficial effects, especially when it is considered how modest and low-cost these interventions are.

Many scholars argue that the weak effects are a result of poor theory. Better theory would lead to stronger effects because it makes the proposed change more plausible and strengthens the link between the nature of the intervention and the psychological mechanism that is going to ensure the change in individual behaviour (Davis et al. 2014). The argument is that the more the intervention is based on good theory the stronger is the effect, though studies of the relationship between theory and effectiveness show mixed results, partly because theory is itself a varied entity, with some theories not being very explicit. Davis and colleagues' review of studies concluded that the problem was not lack of effectiveness, but that the range of theories that are tested is a small subset of a larger number of theories. They suggested that social science and by implication policy-makers are missing out on these potential effects. Nudgers are usually quite cautious and want to deliver a successful result for their clients, often by adding in many mechanisms in a treatment design, making it hard to work out which one is doing the work. Taking the approach of crowding out, too many interventions can reduce the impact of a clear intervention based on one theory. Adding treatments also has the same problems, and may in fact reduce the impact of an intervention. For example, Fieldhouse et al. (2013) tested for different kinds of nudges in their voter turnout experiment, with some households receiving two letters and two telephone calls over successive elections. The treatment arm with the largest number of treatments showed reduced impact compared to treatment arms with fewer interventions.

Moreover, the stronger the insight, the stronger is the effect. It is the case that norms and softer insights have weak effects, but these are never intended to be strong interventions. It is not surprising that effect sizes might be in the 5 per cent range (which yields millions of pounds in revenue in any case). But there are stronger psychological techniques that might be applied, which reach more powerfully into cognition by shaming, making people visible to others, or even making them agitated, all of which are behavioural interventions. In the history of Get-Out-the-Vote studies, there are a number of light-touch strategies that are more about contact than persuasion. They have effect sizes of between 2 and 7 percentage points, with the more personalised interventions yielding the strongest effect, which is consistent with a light-touch behavioural approach (Green and Gerber 2015). If the salience of the psychological device is increased, effect sizes duly improve. In an experiment to test for the impact of exposing a voter to the voting record of neighbours and the record of neighbours back to the voter, Gerber et al. (2008) found that this intervention increased voter turnout by 13 percentage points, a doubling of the treatment effect from more light-touch interventions. By promising to tell respondents the voting history of their neighbours, and the voting history of respondents to the neighbours, researchers can increase turnout from conveying visibility and applying social pressure. The argument is that the reason nudges have been seen to produce what are thought to be relatively low effect sizes is because they have been chosen to be non-controversial. If the nudge unit had chosen stronger interventions the effects would have been greater. It is merely the effect of the choice of instrument, which of course reflects what is acceptable from the sponsoring organisation's point of view and is politically feasible. The nudges that exist are ones that are allowed by policy-makers, not that nudges are necessarily weak treatments. As the rhetoric of behavioural insights is that it is small things that count, it is hardly surprising that that is just what is offered to nudge units to test in interventions. Given that so many resources from government departments are tied up with delivering existing interventions, it is also not surprising that not a huge amount of attention and resources are diverted to delivering behavioural interventions.

TEMPORARY EFFECTS

The third criticism is that nudge policies only have temporary rather than long-lived effects. It is possible for an agency to get an uplift in outcomes but for the change not to be sustained over time. People get excited about changing their behaviours, which lead to an uplift in outcomes, even in the short-term, which makes it look as though a nudge is what was needed; but over time they return to a baseline of habitual behaviours, which is where they want to be in terms of long-term preferences or what suits their lifestyles and that of their peers. This argument comes from the embeddedness claim that people's behaviours are entrenched though their own habits, reinforced by peer-group pressure and social networks, and influenced by the media and the advertising from commercial organisations. This is the argument of Chapter 2. It is easy to see how a small nudge might have only a temporary effect on human behaviour because of these long-term factors. The warm glow given by a nudge can easily fade. People might not even remember the nudge six months after it was given.

One answer is that nudges may be repeated over time, which reflects their low-cost nature. Yet behavioural researchers know that such repeated treatments can fade in effectiveness over time as respondents get used to the nudge. Sometimes nudges depend on novelty, and once they are delivered a few times the effect wears off. Other nudges rely on recipients not knowing they are being nudged. This is because the response needs to be automatic, that is come from unconscious non-reflective processes. If people find out they are being nudged, they will think about it, and they might not like being manipulated. If nudges are repeated over time, they are more likely to be detected. But nudges can be varied, and this is normal practice in the private sector, with companies like Google and Amazon altering their nudges on the basis of feedback and A/B testing. These companies survive and prosper with such strategies.

A more sophisticated idea, which reaches beyond the habit and repetition of nudges, is the claim that nudges can be part of a journey to a new set of outcomes, a way of moving from one equilibrium with negative outcomes for individuals, and the communities of which they are part, to a more positive equilibrium position. At the low equilibrium point behaviours reinforce each other largely as a consequence of the failure of collective action, where it is in nobody's interest to change behaviours, whereas at a more positive equilibrium point, once collective action has been achieved, these positive behaviours reinforce each other, with no one wanting to risk precipitating collective action failure. The nudge then can help citizens solve the collective action problem by conveying signals that encourage others to act. People indicate to one another that they are prepared to do the action. In the words of one report, it is about 'nudging the S-curve', that is affecting the pattern of diffusion and rate of change of adoption (Brook Lyndhurst 2006). This phenomenon links to work on the critical mass whereby there are points of breakthrough in changes in behaviours, and where the nudge might be critical in moving from a slowly rising level of change to one where there is rapid acceleration and norms spread so that everyone adheres to the new desired set of behaviours. As Brook Lyndhurst (2006: 8) reports,

A range of fundamental features of the social system mean that a model of policy intervention predicated on the steady refinement of interventions towards a set of policies that 'work' may be ill-founded. Rather, given the complexities of 'behaviour change', a model of ceaseless innovation, within broad parameters of focus and in a network setting, offers a potentially valuable conceptualisation of how to move forward.

WEAK EXTERNAL VALIDITY

One key criticism of nudge, which relates to other limitations, is the extent to which its findings are transferable to other locations from the places where it has been tested, and that the science of behaviour change is based on a selective reading of the evidence which gives the impression of wide-ranging effects but in fact indicates that the range of subjects upon which it works is limited, partly because of the availability of people to participate in studies. This potential weakness concerns external validity, which is about the ability to generalise. This constraint comes from the fact that most populations for studies are selected to receive the intervention, particularly for more personalised interventions. Because of the need to recruit participants and to get their consent, they are not representative. Marteau et al. (2011: 342) comment on this point: 'To date, few nudging interventions have been evaluated for their effectiveness in changing behaviour in general populations.' Of course, it is possible to sample whole units like local councils, or carry out national evaluations once the pilot has taken place. Fieldhouse et al. (2013) carried out a national-level Get-Out-the-Vote experiment after doing a local intervention (John and Brannan 2008), which allowed them to show the external validity of interventions to all England (Fieldhouse et al. 2014). As nudges become increasingly tested, so more evidence about the range of application of nudges becomes available.

NUDGES DON'T ALWAYS WORK

Linked to the limits of external validity and range is the claim that nudges do not always work in all contexts as expected. Alternatively, the context might be varied just slightly and the nudge yields results that are puzzling or cannot be considered to be the direct result of the research design. A null result from a study does not often give much evidence of why nudges don't work, often just the result, as there are little data to analyse. In the early days of nudge, it seemed that the interventions always worked, such as norms on tax compliance. In fact, examining at the reports of the interventions more closely, such as BIT's work on error and debt (Behavioural Insights Team 2012), shows that not all the interventions worked or worked in the way the behaviourists expected. For example, a BIT trial seeking to impress on doctors that there is a social norm of paying their taxes on time did not work. Another trial sought to replicate Ariely and colleagues' experiment, which asked people to sign an insurance claim at the top rather than at the bottom to prompt the moral nature of the communication, rather than to confirm what had already been written on the form when signed at the bottom (Shu et al. 2012). When trying to replicate the results on prompting people to be honest in declaring whether they had claimed a single-person discount for the local council tax in England, the researchers found the prompt worked best for signing at the bottom rather than the top (Behavioural Insights Team 2012). Norms do not always work when trying to encourage repayment. Silva and John (2017) found that social norms do not encourage students to settle their fees. In another example, Van de Vyver and John (2017) tested for the impact of social norms in seeking to improve the implementation of a government policy that asked local councils and parish councils to register a local community asset, randomly providing half of the councils with social norm information, which did not work either.

In a recent paper, 'Nudges that fail', Sunstein (2017b) draws attention to these negative or null findings, such as information disclosure about the number of calories in an item of food. There are studies showing that placement of food near a checkout can affect choices, but sometimes it does not. Sunstein (2017b) argues that nudges can face the strong counter-preferences of users, which can override defaults. It also seems plausible to suggest that reactance, discussed in Chapter 2, still occurs in reaction to nudges, especially when they are known about by the individuals affected by them. Those who are opposed to the nudges, such as private sector interests, might counter-mobilise, for example banks wanting to keep profitable arrangements when faced with regulations trying to stop them. It is also likely that there are many other nudges that do not work but are not reported. Null findings are hard to publish, and researchers and agencies usually do not want to publicise them. It is impossible to know how many failed nudges there are, in spite of efforts in the major disciplines to encourage the publication of null findings.

Sunstein (2017b) argues for the greater development of stronger nudges and for nudgers not to give up. In particular, better regulation is the answer. Nudges operate better when the grain of public policy changes is in the favoured direction. A more general consideration is that a mature research programme is not dependent on continual successes but needs to learn from failure as part of a genuine desire for reform. If all nudges worked, then there would not be much point in researching them; instead policy-makers should not expect all of them to work, but through failures and successes they can design better nudges and reform wider choice architectures.

WEAK KNOWLEDGE BASE

The irony may be, as Marteau et al. (2011) comment, that nudges have not been evaluated properly in that, although nudges are thought to be cheap, some interventions, such as those on the environment, may be expensive, so are not cost-effective. In spite of the expansion of field trials in this area (see Chapter 5), their number is still relatively low for the purposes of evaluation and cost-benefit analysis. In particular, it is still not possible to do many meta-analyses, which depend on a large number of studies with an identical or similar design. The House of Lords' (2011) report authors commented that their review of the evidence indicated gaps in knowledge in

> aspects of the automatic system, particularly in relation to how emotional processes regulate everyday behaviour; a lack of comparative research into the limits to the transferability of behaviour change interventions across cultural differences; uncertainty about how genes interact with environmental and social factors to cause behaviour; and, a lack of understanding about the effect of social dynamics on behaviour. Other witnesses commented on the challenges involved in integrating the numerous theories of behaviour which were emerging from across the range of sciences of human behaviour. (House of Lords 2011: 17)

Since then, more evidence has appeared on all these aspects of behaviour, but there is not the level of knowledge about the impact of behaviour change that appears in medical evaluations, for example, or in the Campbell Collaboration, which is based on a large number of studies to create meta-analyses.

The claim of lack of evidence, however, is too easily made, as there are always likely to be gaps in knowledge in such a vast field, particularly as behaviour change is a diverse set of activities, with some elements that are relatively new, such as savings and taxation. In all these fields, a large number of studies are emerging, for example studies of norms in public administration settings (see John et al. 2014). The Campbell Collaboration itself reports a large number of behaviour change studies; this increase in reporting reflects the gradual growth of this area in many disciplines, which partly pre-dates the expansion of interest in behavioural economics and the nudge agenda. The interested reader can find reviews of the evidence in such studies as 'Behaviour change programs to prevent HIV among women living in low and middle income countries' (https://www.campbellcollaboration.org/library/women-hiv-behaviour-change-programmes-low-middle-income-countries.html) or 'The effects of school-based social information processing interventions on aggressive behavior: Part I: Universal programs: A systematic review' (https://www.campbellcollaboration.org/website-search?limitstart=20&searchword=behaviour+change), just to name two of the many studies listed on the Campbell Collaboration website. The Behavioural Insights Team website, www.behaviouralinsights.co.uk/, contains summaries of the many studies that have been done by the team. New journals in the field, such as *Behavioural Public Policy* and *Behavioral Science and Policy*, as well as the long-running journals, such as *Behaviour Change*, publish recently-completed studies, which are more than matched by the large research output in journals in established specialist fields, such as *Health Psychology*.

POTENTIALLY HARMFUL

Some critics, such as Marteau et al. (2011), believe that nudges can be harmful. The argument is that conveying light-touch nudges might convince people that some foods are healthy, for example through labelling, and then encourage them to eat more carbohydrates than they should, for example overeating muesli health bars full of honey. Marteau et al. (2011) cite a study of food labels that shows that labels can falsely convey reassurance (Wansink and Chandon 2006). The additional argument that makes this position more decisive is that nudges may not be enough for high-risk individuals or may be artificially reassuring, as what such individuals need is more targeted interventions. This limitation leads to the argument that nudges more generally may not address core behaviours, may prevent individuals from considering the full range of options, and allow them to be reassured by messages that go with the grain of their intuitions. The argument is that individuals might not wish to be confronted with information that they do not like and do not feel comfortable with, or even feel angry about. Getting a more upfront message might cause individuals to reflect upon the problems they face, for only when they have thought about these issues sufficiently can they act. Gentle nudge messages might not be noticed by subpopulations with low education and resources, those people who are focusing on the necessities of life. In short, the argument is that the state should be trying to shove individuals to change their behaviour rather than nudge them.

These arguments on their own do not do enough to knock down nudge. The argument for more targeted interventions for more needy people does not mean that nudges do not work or cannot play a role. The harmful argument does not work here. A more general argument has more merit. This is the idea that encouraging an unreflective process might cause too much dependence and not enough reflection, so nudge is not the solution for long-term problems and might even disguise them. Even if the argument that disguising larger problems might have some force, it does not show that nudges are harmful. A lot depends on the kind of nudge, and the nudge could conceivably be the first step to wider reflections by individuals, with the nudge being the precipitator rather than the obstacle. It is a hard argument to sustain that the nudge could harm the individual's ability to receive a welfare-enhancing message, having a kind of soporific effect.

DIVERTING PUBLIC ATTENTION

Even mainstream authors in behavioural science (e.g. Marteau et al. 2011) as well as critics (Goodwin 2012) have come to believe that the use of behavioural sciences in government and the rise of behavioural policies has de-privileged more interventionist policies on the part of government. Stressing light-touch, non-regulatory, and fiscally cheap policies, diverts public attention from the tools and measures that are more effective. This was the view of a critical government report from the UK House of Lords (2011). This criticism is partly a function of a restrictive focus on nudge: 'interventions which may be described as "nudging" are not synonymous with, but rather are a subset of, non-regulatory interventions' (House of Lords 2011: 12). As was argued in Chapters 3 and 4, this is an overly restrictive view of nudging which means that many of the customisations of tougher policy instruments would be ruled out. While nudges are cheap to do, nudge is not going to rule out another strategy. In fact, nudging works well in combination with standard approaches to effecting change, except that what behavioural insights offer is the chance to make the policy work in a better way. The policy-maker gets all the advantages of the existing tools of government with their proven advantages but with all the added value of behavioural insights.

It is not plausible to argue that the state is locked into a set of activities that rule out either nudges or more stronger interventions. It would be different if the two strategies cost a lot of money and nudges were marginally cheaper, encouraging government to go for them. Of course, it is still possible that governments face limits to the use of resources, so it could be the case that if the cost per outcome was significantly in nudge's favour it would lead to a redistribution of resources away from in-depth interventions to more population-based ones. This does not pose a large problem in the efficient allocation of government resources, because society benefits. Government might want to weight the targeted resources to ensure that needy individuals were protected, but even this would not deny the argument that nudge and targeted strategies are complementary and that a government might want to find the efficient balance between the two.

The critical argument can, however, go further. The critic knows that the government will not be rational in allocating its time, but in fact the government might be under different kinds of pressure. One might be to cut resources generally. The availability of a cheap measure would appear to satisfy a government that it was meeting a need so could justify cuts made to more targeted and expensive interventions elsewhere. A government might have an ideological preference to cut back the state, and the nudge strategy might give it the ability to do that, because it depends on a light-touch intervention that does not affect the autonomy of the individual. In this view, nudge plays into a right-wing agenda while appearing neutral and pleasing to all. Appearing shiny and new, it can be a cover for worse things happening.

This argument again rests on nudge taking a particular form, that is favouring only light-touch techniques, but it can just as easily be used to favour stronger interventions done in a nudge way. When seen in this way, there is no political project behind nudge: it is neutral, really about implementation, not making policy choices and does not rule out certain kinds of choice. The fact that a government of the right chose nudge in a period of fiscal austerity might show enthusiasm for low-cost approaches; but, in fact, as Chapter 5 shows, it owed more to timing and context as behavioural approaches had become fashionable, when policy entrepreneurs were at work in and around government, and that the prime minister, David Cameron, happened to have a social agenda which was about promoting good behaviour and better collective outcomes, which worked well with nudges. In other parts of the world, such as the Netherlands and the USA, the agenda was taken up by non-right-wing governments; and even right-wing governments, such as those led by Theresa May or Donald Trump, are not guaranteed to like nudge. It does not fit into a simple political box.

LIMITS TO INCREMENTALISM

In essence, the behaviour change programme is not about a radical overhaul of public policy, as it relies on a series of tweaks to the policy-making process. It does not impose a rationalist vision upon the policy-maker, and produces more responsive and considered policies as a result. This is incrementalism, an approach to policy-making that the Behavioural Insights Team celebrates (Halpern and Mason 2015), in particular a version called 'radical incrementalism', the idea that through many small steps radical transformation may come about.

The use of this term draws attention to a familiar debate in public policy, studied first in the 1950s (to which starting students of public policy are introduced in their first weeks of study). A number of influential public policy scholars argued that the incremental pattern of decision-making, that of making a series of experimental small steps and then learning based upon experience, creates an adaptive kind of governance, which draws upon the knowledge of organisations and their competing elements, and celebrates a decentralised approach to decision-making. Even the term 'radical incrementalism' has a long pedigree, going back to at least the 1960s (Wildavsky 1966). Lindblom argued strongly for an incremental approach to policy-making (Lindblom 1959, 1965; Braybrooke and Lindblom 1963), which has been contested on both empirical and normative grounds ever since. On empirical grounds, it has been observed that such a stepped approach to decision-making is not how modern democracies work, as they often have long periods when not much happens, followed by rapid changes or policy punctuations (Baumgartner and Jones 1993; Jones and Baumgartner 2005). If these ideas about policy-making are taken as read, then the incremental approach is not in the grain of how decision-makers operate in that reformers need to be aware that they are at their most powerful when a new regime starts to change, and the reforms and changes can start to happen quickly, reinforced by media and political interest, which causes a radical rethink of routines and existing policy choices. Simply burrowing up from below will not transform public policy. Nudge is likely to receive resistance from within bureaucracies, and also supporters in the wider policy community, who will not support such changes without an agenda shift. Radical incrementalism in this view does not work.

The other critical point of view, is best summarised in the critique of Goodin (1982). He argues that policy-makers do not want incrementalism, as it does not provide a route map of where they want to go.

Incremental decision-making could lead to cliff edges without the policy-makers knowing they are there, or have sleeper effects which are negative but which are not realised in a series of incremental gains, each of which looks plausible and beneficial but where all get worse off in the long run.

Of course, there are easy ripostes to these points of view. For the empirical critiques, even the policy agendas and punctuated equilibrium perspectives do not rule out some form of incrementalism in periods of slow change. Moreover, advocates of this perspective often acknowledge the beginning of changes in an approach during the period of stability whereby old ways of doing things do not work. As incremental changes do not offer benefits in the same way as before, policy-makers start to learn that, even though there may be strong upswings in attention, these are often based on a lot of groundwork beforehand. In this way, the use of behavioural insights can be the baseline and a form of preparation for radical changes that can get unleashed. If bureaucracies do become more experimental and willing to try out new measures, the expectation is that for much of the period not much happens, but then this very experimentation can contribute to the radical changes happening later on. In terms of the normative critique, this criticism also depends on a characterisation of incrementalist decision-making as a completely blind set of policies, which is not a realistic position to adopt. Just as much intelligence and guidance can apply to decision-making under incrementalism, which can resemble rational action; it is just that the means of getting to decisions is different. Incremental decision-makers can review their options, look forwards and backwards, even if the overall strategy is adaptive. In fact, blindness is more associated with rational decisions, trusting the policy analysis or consultant's report, rather than incrementalism, which is more about responsiveness and gaming the environment. The critique of radical incrementalism fails.

IDEOLOGICAL AND NEOLIBERAL

Another type of criticism comes from within social science, from researchers interested in the politics of knowledge and its use. It concerns the use of psychology in government, which is thought to be manipulative and to exclude more political underpinnings of government intervention (e.g. Jones et al. 2013). In part, this critique of nudge policies relies on accepting a number of other claims, one of which is that modern politics and policy are characterised by an ideology, that of neoliberalism, which is a set of ideas that legitimate market institutions, and that reproduce over time in ways that extend individualist and market-orientated thinking (see Jones et al. 2013: 6). The way in which nudge emerges does not lead to the consideration of more radical solutions to policy problems. The approach to public policy tends to focus on the individual causes of policy problems rather than the wider structural reasons linked to the operation of a market economy. Nudge posits a public policy response based on influencing individual choices. This chimes with the views of other critics, like Dobson (2011), who criticises nudge for its de-politicisation and neglect of the wider context of political debates, such as green nudges that do not consider the wider reasons for environmental problems. This involves denying the ethical foundation of these debates:

> In thinking of sustainability as a matter of tweaking behaviour, nudgers commit what philosophers call a 'category mistake'. Ethics, norms and values are not an optional extra in sustainability – they are constitutive of it. From this point of view, it is as absurd to see sustainability as a matter of resizing waste bins as it would have been to nudge slave owners towards ending slavery by making their ships a little shorter and narrower. (Dobson 2011: 9)

Of course, there are problems with this argument in that nudge may be seen to be partly a critique of those same market-driven policies, which are based on rational calculations, whereas behavioural economists want to move beyond this. Jones et al. (2013: 10) argue that Kahneman and Tversky's work 'embodies a normative assumption of rationality', which seems to go too far and does not appear to do them justice, as many behavioural economists, such as Sugden, do not operate with strict rational assumptions. A neoliberal argument would regard behavioural economics as critical of the economics of the new right and questioning of the rational model. This blunderbuss approach is the main problem with these functionalist arguments in that any government policy can be fashioned to be seen to support an existing order, when in fact ideas and policies may be independent and different from each other. For example, it is possible to imagine a socialist state with no market mechanisms suffering from a weakness of internal commands and needing a nudge-based policy to improve them. Nudge might in fact be more important in a centralised or market-constrained economy, as there is a need to motivate citizens to act with a less clear perception of the reward. In market societies, given how long nudge has been used by the private sector, the use of it by the public sector may be regarded as a reclaiming of these techniques for public purposes, again the antithesis of a neoliberal approach. After all, the big criticism of nudge from libertarians is that it is paternalist, not that it is libertarian (see Chapter 7 on ethics).

An acceptance of the lack of stable preferences as implied in behavioural economics may suggest that the state should not intervene (see Sugden 2008), but it can also mean that policy-makers need to pay more attention to the general design of policies and the constitutional issues governing their operation. As Hargreaves-Heap (2017: 10) writes, 'behavioural public policy should also be concerned with the character of constitutional rules that constrain and enable action'. Once the unstable nature of preferences is considered, it justifies a more egalitarian approach to state intervention, such as for taxes and benefits, so that people's interests are protected.

That is not to say there is not conservatism within the behavioural programme, as was recounted in Chapters 3 and 4, in that potentially radical ideas became integrated within mainstream economics, and also were fashioned in a way that could respond to the concerns of policy-makers. Even though much customisation of academic ideas had occurred, this is a different argument to saying that nudge is a manifestation of neoliberalism. Within nudge there are radical ideas that do not sit with the existing order, which can build on the work that has been done, which in effect is what Jones et al. (2013) are arguing. The difference with the position adopted here is that more agency should be attributed to the ideas and people involved so the policies do not result necessarily from an all-encompassing ideology. By introducing the overarching set of ideas from Foucault, the analysis becomes rather determinist. It seems a better course to say that ideas emerged where they were consistent with the existing order, but that their radicalism remained intact waiting to be rediscovered, which Jones et al. (2013) hint at in their concluding chapter. Overall, the difference between Jones et al. (2013) and the position here is that the Foucauldian approach does not give enough emphasis to the agency of the actors involved in the policy process. The argument in Chapter 8 points out that a technocratic and top-down approach to behavioural policy is not a necessary consequence of its adoption, but that a more decentralised and open approach can be adopted whereby a range of actors can use these ideas. Agency is the way forward.

NEGLECTING CITIZEN INTELLIGENCE AND FEEDBACK

The final criticism links to these earlier points, but is more specific. This is the idea that nudge policies do not take advantage of citizen involvement and feedback, because of the nature of nudge policies, which are designed behind closed doors, particularly if the nudges only work if they are kept secret from the citizens so that citizens do not get the chance to be involved. This means that designers of behavioural public policies do not take advantage of the correction of errors and feedback. As Farrell and Shalizi (2011) write, 'There is no reason to think technocrats know better, especially since Thaler and Sunstein offer no means for ordinary people to comment on, let alone correct, the technocrats' prescriptions. This leaves the technocrats with no systematic way of detecting their own errors, correcting them, or learning from them.'

It is commonly assumed that nudge policies can only work if kept secret, but this is not right. People often like being nudged, and this is the whole point of the Thaler and Sunstein agenda: that people have preferences to do good things or to help themselves in the long term. They even want to be nudged. It is a way to get to their good selves. If the large amount of public opinion evidence that Sunstein (2016) has collected is accepted, citizens approve of and welcome nudge policies, which means that if they realise they are being nudged this might even improve the chances that policies might be accepted. Even though nudges work on the non-reflective and automatic systems, it is possible to consider a stage of reflection that might accompany or reinforce these automatic system-based processes (see the argument in Chapter 8). There might be a realisation that a nudge has taken place, which might help the individual keep on track afterwards and put in place plans to keep the good behaviour going. This might become an automatic and self-regulating process later on when the individual does not need to think about the new set of behaviours.

There is nothing to stop nudges involving citizen contact and feedback, and incorporating more democratic processes, which is implied by the public nature of nudging and that there are public good aspects to what is being influenced. This view is closer to the world of Ostrom (1990) and supports self-reinforcing forms of governance rather than the science of manipulation. But there is some truth to the criticism based on observation of how nudge is currently practised. It is mainly technocratic, carried out by administrators advised by behavioural scientists who use randomised controlled trials to select the best option. Although nudges are usually approved by political principals and they are not done in secret, they are introduced without a lot of public involvement or wider debate, even in the bureaucracy, as well as in other democratic forums. Most nudges are not done in consultation with citizens, do not involve feedback whereby citizen views can be incorporated.

The argument that nudges could be widened to take account of this criticism was made in *Nudge, Nudge, Think, Think* (John et al. 2011).

That book suggested there are two traditions of examining citizen roles in public policy, the nudge route and the think route, the latter drawing on ideas in deliberative democracy. These ideas are regarded as opposites, as they draw from different intellectual traditions, so might not appear to be comparable. The two traditions are closer than might be imagined, partly because successful nudging will involve some reflection and understanding of the wider policy issues. Deliberation, which has been limited in the way in which it has been implemented in recent years because of self-selection by and inequalities among citizens, needs to be made more practical and egalitarian. The use of behavioural ideas can encourage some reflection as part of a nudge-based intervention, and where all citizens can be encouraged to think. More of this argument appears later in the book, especially in Chapter 8.

CONCLUSION

Nudge has attracted criticism from all quarters, which is entirely to be expected given it is an idea and set of policies popular with policy-makers and experts, and that a lot is claimed from the approach. Academics and critics like to knock new approaches down, so the question becomes how much do these criticisms hold, and whether they imply limitations to the range of nudges that can be used, which brings the argument to the question and title of this book. If all these criticisms are taken seriously, they would severely limit how far to nudge. Of course, often it is a question of degree, because it is hard to see that there are fundamental objections to nudge, in the sense that these policies must have some use and that few people can disagree with measures that improve the payment of taxes and achievement of other desirable outcomes, especially as they are low-cost and unobtrusive. It would take someone of a very critical turn of mind to see such measures as conspiratorial and ideological, having poor long-term consequences for political action, and increasing citizen passivity. Even critics such as Marteau et al. (2011) do not go that far, nor do those writing from a critical perspective (e.g. Jones et al. 2013) who are sceptical about the current manifestation of nudge rather than believe it is necessarily bad.

The key question is about limits – the range of applications, weak effect sizes, and longevity. These factors appear to relegate nudges to a useful but limited range of applications which do not add very much to the conventional tools of government. Nudges from this viewpoint do not address the fundamental causes of behaviours and moreover cannot address them. This is the argument considered in the first half of this chapter. Even though it is possible to see some truths to this criticism, overall it is a misconceived position, partly because it is based on what is easily observed in the current wave of changes and ignores the power of behavioural interventions as they are developing currently. It also fails to appreciate the key idea behind behavioural interventions, which is the rooting of public action in an understanding of the cognitions of citizens and helping them work through their constraints. The critique is based on a false conception of nudge: that behavioural public policy is limited just to light-touch interventions. Instead most public actions may be shaped by behavioural science and improved by a better understanding of individual cognitions. It so happens that thinking through these limitations and cognitions does encourage a gentler, more decentralised, and human-centric form of governance, but this is not something that automatically follows from altering choice architectures.

The more conceptual critiques rest and fall on their own premises. If the taste is for the psychological state then the modest interventions that make up nudge are going to confirm this approach no matter how they are introduced. But it is hard to support the idea of the psychological state from the way in which these interventions have been introduced. Nudge adoptions reflect the pluralism of central state organisations. They tend to be patchily introduced, even though they can be transformative. Behavioural insights and randomised controlled trials have largely been introduced in an open and transparent way, which does not conform to the image of psychologists secretly using their power to manipulate citizens for government ends. In practice, the nudge agenda has emerged with a lot of public attention, rather than the secret state taking control. The same can be said for other critiques, which are about diverting attention from the so-called serious tools of government, as there is no evidence that this has taken place as a result of nudge. It is not possible to prove the assertion that more nudge equals less regulation, even though certain governments may have said that. Nudge works well for both left and right, and for governments of any complexion. It is mainly neutral, merely saying that the designers of any intervention need to consider carefully how largely autonomous social and economic actors are going to respond to the sanction or request. It can make governments of the left, the centre, and the right more agile and effective. Nothing is ruled in or out in behavioural public policy, at least only in terms of practicability. Of course, the policy-maker may wish to rule out certain activities on ethical grounds, which is the topic of the next chapter.

7. The ethics of nudge

An important consideration for how far to nudge, which goes beyond practicability and effectiveness, is moral and ethical constraints. Nudge policies might work, but governments should not use them if they offend moral values, are inconsistent with other values that are important to uphold, or have negative effects on achieving other important objectives that are based on following ethical standards. There is some overlap with the criticisms of the psychological state, discussed in Chapter 6, in arguments about loss of autonomy, but considerations about ethics move the debate more toward the realm of philosophy and moral argument, so they deserve a separate chapter.

Nudge has attracted a lot of argument in this vein, partly because its advocates Thaler and Sunstein made great play of the term 'libertarian paternalism', which implies that policies that are carried out in the interests of the citizens without their consent could at the same time uphold their freedom. As Thaler and Sunstein realise, this is a controversial position to hold, and arguments for and against it are reviewed in this chapter. In the end, this book's argument is that it is better to accept that nudge can at times be paternalist, but that paternalism is not necessarily an ethically problematic position to hold. It might be acceptable or ethically defensible to constrain freedom in certain circumstances, provided various safeguards have been implemented, so that extreme or controversial interventions have been ruled out or modified. There are different ways of being paternalist, some of which uphold citizen consent and legitimacy in a democratic state, and they can form into a fruitful line of interventions in behavioural public policy.

It matters ethically whether the decision-making before the nudge was carried out following democratic procedures and was fully transparent. As nudges are directed to all the tools of government, thus affecting the design of all or most public policies, they involve the same considerations on human freedom as increasing taxes, introducing new laws, and even going to war, in that democratically agreed policies that respect human rights can be followed if there is enough provision for their review and their effectiveness is demonstrable. In this sense, the argument in this chapter is that the debate about libertarian paternalism is a red herring or diversion. That is not to say there are not moral arguments to consider, or that respecting human choice cannot be beneficial in some nudge policies, but getting beyond this debate is useful because it allows academics and policy-makers to focus on issues that are of more importance and can help guide citizens to make better choices in public policy. Moreover, the debate about libertarian paternalism disguises other ethical questions about the use of the tools of behavioural public policy. Questions of the desirability of manipulation come to the fore, as does the question of when deception and secrecy might be sanctioned, or when some degree of anxiety or harm caused by an intervention can be justified, or whether there are some nudges that are off limits to the policy-maker and researcher. The debate about ethics and nudges involves considering wider questions about the ethical constraints on public action, and on the correct use of research to gain knowledge from human subjects.

LIBERTARIAN PATERNALISM

The starting point for discussions of the ethics of nudge is libertarian paternalism. Thaler and Sunstein (2008; see also Camerer et al. 2003) argued for this position as a way to justify the extensive use of behavioural interventions. The authors recognised that the term could be seen as an oxymoron, as it appears contradictory: how could something be paternalistic, which is about taking away autonomy, making a decision in place of people acting purely on their own, but at the same time be libertarian, where individuals are free from constraint to follow their preferences and tastes no matter what the consequences are for them? Although apparently contradictory, it is possible to defend this position.

The basic idea behind the libertarian paternalist argument is that individuals are free not to follow a nudge and to take the opposite action if they decide to do so. The whole set-up behind a default encourages this. For example, the driver licensing website that prompts organ donation, or even defaults to that choice if individuals take no action, may be designed so people are free to reject the prompt or default and with relatively little cost choose the option that they want so as to satisfy their preferences. The paternalistic side is that the public authority is hinting or arranging matters to influence the choices of individuals, so that they end up choosing the one that is socially desirable and/or better for them, perhaps unconsciously or by being prompted to do so. There is a real-world influence of the state and public authority, as the whole point of the evidence for nudge, as reviewed in the previous chapters, is that the message and its framing matter. People do change their behaviour as a consequence of nudges, so their choices are being affected by what people in public office decide. But as choice is respected as well as being influenced so there is libertarian paternalism: 'choice architects can preserve freedom of choice while also nudging people in directions that will improve their lives' (Thaler and Sunstein 2008: 252).

One key issue in the use of behavioural science – and one that becomes important when reflecting on think later in the book – is the extent to which people are consciously exercising their freedom when responding to a nudge. For the libertarian, it matters that individuals are aware of the choice being offered. If the nudge is designed to prevent such awareness emerging, or working entirely automatically, it is hard to see it as an exercise of free choice. Nudge advocates defend the use of automatic processes because if individuals did reflect on their choices and agreed with them, and might even have been trying to achieve the outcome and failed, they would probably thank the public officials for making the choice easy for them. Officials can say that rather than overriding freedom the public authority is removing the framing biases that limit making effective choices.

This argument becomes one of the selling points about nudge in that people's freedom is respected. Light-touch policies can be used by politicians who do not want to intrude on people's liberty, for example avoiding a policy of banning some food or regulating its content. This characteristic has the advantage of building support for nudge and creating the conditions for successful policies. The light-touch nature of nudge affects the ethical justification of nudge in that these policies may have more legitimacy and acceptability.

It is possible to attack libertarian paternalism because even soft paternalism requires some constraint on autonomy. If people are short of time, they don't have the opportunity to reflect on all the choices. If government limits the information upon which choices are based and individuals do not have enough resources to challenge the decision, the effect is just as if the proposal had been mandatory. Had people been offered a more balanced choice, leading to a more active decision on their part, they could have made a freer selection of their course of action.

There is also a defence of more libertarian arrangements even when there are human biases. Some economists, such as Sugden (2008), claim that markets can organise themselves even with incoherent individual preferences and still generate welfare gains. Sugden takes the view that the argument of libertarian paternalism makes an assumption that people are rational underneath, merely that they have been diverted from their true interests by biases. But this reasoning is contrary to the findings of behavioural economics, which does not always assume that rationality operates fully in the first place. It is just not clear what the true preferences of citizen actors are, so lack of certainty weakens the justification for the paternalist claim for overriding them. The implication is that there is no planner underneath the doer. From this perspective, it is not coherent for the state to override preferences as if there were market failure. Sugden's position is that overriding those preferences limits freedom as much as in classic paternalism.

Much turns on the term paternalism. Its use by Thaler and Sunstein is thought to be ambiguous (Sugden 2016), wandering between what people would choose for themselves and what is good for them. Moreover, as Sugden writes,

> *self-acknowledged* self-control problems are a lot less common than many behavioural economists seem to think. Even if behavioural economists or policy makers feel confident that people's lifestyle choices are based on some kind of error, they should not jump to the conclusion that the error is a self-acknowledged failure of self-control, or that (as Thaler puts it) it is what those people would *themselves call* an error. (Sugden 2016: 122, italics in original)

These nudges are turning what affects a small number of people and their actions into a more general constraint on human action.

It is hard to defend the libertarian aspect of libertarian paternalism when libertarians say that the whole point of freedom is the latitude to make bad choices if that is what people want to do. It is a hard argument for nudge advocates to extract themselves out of. Thaler and Sunstein try by referring to the duty to explain things to people, so if a government knows that an activity is bad it must explain this. One way of thinking about this problem is to consider a public information sign warning people of a cliff edge, which might appear to be paternalistic (similar examples appear in Mill, and it is also the argument made by Dworkin (1988) that government can act in the case of insanity), but is placed in a prominent position to nudge people not to go further; they are nevertheless free to take the risk. As Anderson (2010: 372) notes, 'the appeal to soft paternalism will work for Thaler and Sunstein only if all choice-improving nudges are to be understood along the lines of misinformation and temporary insanity'. But, of course, that is not the case, as most people have some freedom and rationality, even if they do not exercise them at all times. Many situations make less clear what is the legitimate role of the state.

Thaler and Sunstein are also vulnerable to an attack that freedom has been limited by the nudge itself. Citizens were not free to choose an alternative option because the choice architecture guided them subconsciously to the government's ends. When delivering behavioural public policy, the decision-maker cannot realistically inform the citizen at the point of decision, either in terms of the effectiveness of the nudge or delivering a reflective choice, for example, at the point of say donating organs (though, as this book argues, this can be improved). The whole point is that the opportunity to nudge needs to be wrapped up with other procedures, such as a standard letter or the design of a website, and nudges needs to work quickly, easily, and automatically. This point relates to a more general criticism of nudge, that it is manipulative and autonomy limiting through using psychological techniques (e.g. Mols et al. 2015).

To get out of the problem that the practice of nudge appears to limit choices as they are being made, and that consent cannot be sought, Thaler and Sunstein (2008: 244) argue for the publicity principle that 'bans government from selecting a policy that it would not be willing to defend publicly to its citizens'. They hold back from making all nudges public at the point of carrying them out, saying that many nudges work best when focused on automatic processes. Their proposal respects citizens by policy-makers being willing to argue for the benefits subsequently. These are dangerous waters, as Thaler and Sunstein well know, and amount to an after-the-event justification, like for secrecy. The moral force of an argument does not depend on when it has happened: it should apply both beforehand and afterwards. As Anderson writes, it puts them in the company of planners who say about their decisions that no one will really mind. He goes on to write: 'the espousal of transparency and publicity constraints comes across as an artificial and ad hoc declaration of values that belies a lack of real interest in the importance of ensuring that those subjected to these subtle forms of state power understand the underlying rationale' (Anderson 2010: 374). Even if people agree with the decisions, they often like process to be followed and to be consulted in any case. Part of the problem is that almost anything can conceivably be justified after the event. Most writers and thinkers know that sophisticated arguments can be put forward for almost any position, but this is not the same as arguing face-to-face with citizens to justify their restriction of choice.

Thaler and Sunstein (2008) also face a cliff-edge argument of their own, as they acknowledge that there is nothing to stop any infringement of the liberty of the citizen from being seen as a nudge: there is no hard-and-fast distinction between hard and soft paternalism. Anticipating this argument, Thaler and Sunstein (2008) argue that difficult cases emerge and can be dealt with by additional procedures for consideration. It might be said in their defence that public policy is full of these balancing decisions where no outcome perfectly respects one principle, but where policy-makers need to make the best choice that maximises their values and ensures the policy does not lead to perverse effects. There is no slippery slope, providing good reasoning has been undertaken.

One strong argument for defending the claims about freedom is that choice is anyway constrained by government policies and a range of private sector interventions, as well as by social institutions. As Thaler and Sunstein (2008: 252) write, 'nudges are everywhere, even if we do not see them'. Liberals have classically argued against libertarians, such as Nozick (1974), that there is no first state of liberty from which an intervention or law removes freedom. Whatever a public agency does, whether to nudge or not to nudge, affects freedom. Choice architectures have to be created whatever the public agency does. The question is whether they are designed with the right choices embodied in them.

In the view of critics, in spite of all the gentleness of nudge, there is no getting away from the fact that nudges deprive individuals of their autonomy or do not respect individuals' full autonomy. The objection, as Anderson (2010: 374) writes, 'concerns the marginal status of respect for the autonomy of those targeted for nudges'. There is an elite whose members make decisions that affect others. It might be more straight-forward just to argue for a strong paternalist policy to justify this ethically, as Conly (2013) does on the basis of a duty to prevent harm.

But can a version of the autonomy argument work when delivering nudges? Given the reality of policy-making and modern society where citizens are busy with their own lives, pay taxes, and delegate decisions about welfare to politicians who run expert and professionalised bureau-cracies, some notion of encouraging the full autonomy of citizens to own the nudges and to debate them is not realistic, but the question is whether the balance could be tipped a little bit in the direction of citizen control and autonomy. There may be some halfway house between secretive nudging and full-scale deliberation: 'a choice architecture that makes it easier to avoid regrettable decisions or, rather, various measures to improve individuals' decision-making capacities, say, through education, "buddy" arrangements, decision-making heuristics, etc.' (Anderson 2009: 375). It is instructive that one of the limiting conditions that Thaler and Sunstein (2008) offer is the chance for citizens to be given an opportunity to think and reflect before they make a bad choice. The authors get closer to the deliberative nudges favoured in this book, and Chapter 8 suggests a way forward.

FREEDOM AND THE PSYCHOLOGICAL STATE

One consideration is whether the behavioural sciences, in particular those that rest on cognitive science, have re-orientated the role of the state to take greater power over the citizen based on detailed knowledge about individual behaviour and how to manipulate it. This argument appears, as was discussed in Chapter 6, in the concept of the psychological state (Jones et al. 2013), which implies that more harnessing of behavioural sciences may reduce autonomy and freedom. There is a kind of technological argument at work here, which is that former sorts of authority were not efficient and could not control individual behaviour effectively. Citizens benefited from a degree of inefficacy in government bureaucracies that worked with imperfect knowledge. The argument about behaviour change knowledge is that it can realise the Weberian ideal of the rational bureaucracy that oppresses freedom, much as Weber feared. This argument depends on a degree of homogeneity which it is hard for any scientific programme to achieve, let alone the diverse field of behavioural sciences, not least because it has not been fully adopted and the same messy bureaucratic structures and involvement of politicians and many other actors are all in play, as discussed in Chapter 5. In short, the use of different forms of knowledge is an important development, but it cannot be seen to be a step-change in the dominance of knowledge that the argument about the psychological state implies. The argument is also that certain categories of people are subject to behaviour change interventions, which may not be true; and, in any case, certain categories of people, notably the poor, have always been on the receiving end of government policies and research efforts, such as those who are on welfare. Nudge is no different in that respect. And a lot of nudges are applied to the whole population, such as tax reminders or organ donation prompts. Of course, everyone is in receipt of nudges from the private sector, such as marketing, advertising, social media content, and television campaigns.

As Thaler and Sunstein (2008) argue, much depends on the neutrality of the policy-makers and the proposals they advocate. If nudges have a political angle or are ideological or are about imposing the preferences of policy-makers for a particular way of life, then nudges are doomed. It gets worse if the policy-maker advances what may be considered to be bad objectives from nudges, such as reducing the influence of political opponents, or getting re-elected. This is one of the key worries about nudging; as Schmidt (2017: 406) argues, 'the granting the state the power to systematically nudge its citizens indeed puts some people in a position to impose their will on others'.

It is possible to sustain this argument by referring to the arguments of the previous chapters, in that nudges have appeared from scientific investigations and so are evidenced by social scientists, based on research from trials. Moreover, the objectives of nudge policies, at least in their first wave, are ones that few will object to, such as paying taxes on time or improving health outcomes. Moreover, the nudge argument implies some faith in the political process in that citizens expect that politicians are there for the public interest and bureaucrats want to improve outcomes. The democratic state has as part of its function the improvement of welfare, and that public officials are motivated by a public service motivation, for which there is some evidence as witnessed by surveys. When taking into account the power of the private sector, which has no clear path of democratic accountability in spite of progress on corporate governance, to use nudges which are not designed to be in the public interest but to make profit, objections to democratically controlled nudges weaken. The contrast between using nudges in the private sector, where the consumer can usually exit from the provider using nudges, and the situation of no exit from the monopoly state does not apply, because the consumer might be genuinely unaware of the nudges in the private sector, but it is possible to find out about public sector nudges (Schmidt 2017: 415).

On the other hand, politicians do authorise some policies to get re-elected, bureaucrats act from self-interest as well, and private interests sometimes capture bureaucrats, a point acknowledged by Thaler and Sunstein (2008: 240). This lapsing from a generally good path is another reason to argue for more accountable nudging, which is done in public so that the actions can be properly scrutinised, not to establish after the event whether people would have agreed with them. In part, the slightly ambiguous text at the conclusion of *Nudge* (Thaler and Sunstein 2008) supports such an open process.

SUNSTEIN'S LATER ARGUMENTS

In later books, Sunstein elaborates on his defence of libertarian paternalism. In *Why Nudge?* (2014a), he argues strongly against the limitations of Mill's harm principle, which justifies limits on freedom if actions harm others. He argues that Mill was writing when it seemed reasonable to leave people to their own actions, based on rational self-assessment. With social science research, it is now known that people make massive errors when they make judgements. That provides the justification for intervening. Just as there is a justification for the state intervening in market failure, so it is legitimate for the state to intervene in what he calls 'behavioural market failure'. Mill in any case provided a justification for overriding preferences in the case of children or so-called primitive peoples. Sunstein holds back from saying these behavioural biases are a good reason to be paternalistic on their own, as other reasoning needs to be engaged in, but it is a good starting point. Sunstein still defends nudges as superior, as they are liberty-enhancing, defending what he calls 'soft paternalism' against a harder kind. Of course, as Sunstein realises, the distinction has its problems, not least the lack of a clear division between the different kinds of paternalism and the possibility of slippage between them. But he defends a welfare-enhancing policy in the form of soft nudges, particularly if welfare is seen in a broad sense.

These ideas are picked up in *The Ethics of Influence* (Sunstein 2016), which summarises his earlier position that 'ethical issues largely turn on whether nudges promote or instead undermine welfare, autonomy, dignity, and self-government' (Sunstein 2016: 11). A government might in fact have an ethical obligation to nudge to prevent disease and to stop people acting in bad ways. The arguments are similar to those for the use of other tools of government, such as fines, which is close to the position adopted in the summary below. At times nudging might undermine people's dignity, so it might be right not to do it, such as if people feel tricked by the nudge. For example, the social pressure argument of exposing voter turnout to neighbours might not be the right way to mobilise citizens to turn out at the polls (Gerber et al. 2008). Overall, public officials should aim to be trustworthy to build trust with the citizens when executing nudges, as they are expected to be more generally.

There is still the preference for choice-enhancing interventions, but the defence is less strong on libertarian grounds than in *Nudge* (Thaler and Sunstein 2008), which is entirely understandable given the attacks that have been made against libertarian paternalism even though Sunstein still keeps an element of this earlier defence. He maintains his view that there are already many nudges in operation, which means that government is simply replacing one nudge with another. He makes an argument for deciding the moral content of nudges on a case-by-case basis. The promotion of autonomy is an important goal. In fact, many nudges do promote reflection and are essentially educative (Sunstein 2017a).

Sunstein (2016) still prefers defaults to more active choices, at least in some circumstances, where people have very low knowledge about the choice and thinking about policies is difficult. In these cases, defaults are better. Manipulation is not to be approved of, largely because of the ends to which manipulation is targeted, and that individuals would not on reflection agree with the position advocated. Most nudges pass through the manipulation test, but not all do, and some are on the borderline. Here there is a more complex debate to be had.

PUBLIC OPINION AND NUDGING

Sunstein's (2017a) book has a chapter on public opinion and nudging, which is about whether people like nudging, that in the main they do as they approve of these policies (see also Hagman et al. 2015). Ultimately, as Sunstein fully realises, ethical arguments do not turn on public opinion. Just because the public approves of the policy does not make it right. But the findings help the arguments that Sunstein wishes to make. If the public really disapproved of nudges then it could be argued that they were manipulated, as on reflection they would not agree with the interventions; but approval indicates that they would not mind too much being nudged and approve of the arguments for promoting behaviour change, giving some support to Sunstein's position. Of course, it is important to be cautious about public opinion, in that such answers might not be the consequence of much reflection, and that opinion poll responses can be framed by the question wording. But this reservation can be assuaged by the basic finding that people agree with nudges if they approve of the end being promulgated. The main difference is that partisan affiliation affects the approval rating, which indicates that ideology may play a role, undermining in part the neutrality criterion in nudge.

Other distinctions in the willingness of the public to approve nudge appear in Jung and Mellers's (2016) study, which manipulates frames as well as tests for support. The authors focus on whether the nudge is stated up front and is overt, or whether it is covert and subconscious, which replicates the distinction between system 1 and system 2 forms of decision-making. Unsurprisingly the US public tend to favour the more overt kind, which supports the think approach to nudging argued for in Chapter 8 (see also Felsen et al. 2013). People also prefer the pro-social nudges to the more pro-self ones. Those that are preferred are about collective benefit, such as recycling and other collective goods. The less paternalistic nudges get more approval from citizens. Overall the vast majority of nudges were supported in this study. Political views also condition the acceptability of nudges. The responsiveness to nudges shows considerable heterogeneity, whereby some people are more susceptible to nudges than others, while some show reactance. As in Sunstein's approach, the acceptability of nudges is altered if they are personalised, suggesting a future direction for the design of nudges.

The heterogeneity is not just limited to type of person but may vary cross-nationally, which may affect the extent to which policy-makers can justify nudges to their citizens. Petrescu et al. (2016) also manipulated the information conveyed, finding that the acceptability of limiting portion size was less acceptable in the USA than in the UK (any UK person who has visited a US restaurant away from the metropolitan centres won't be surprised by this conclusion), though there was no difference for other government interventions to reduce consumption of sugar-sweetened beverages. In this study, education was preferred to regulation, with support for nudges somewhere in between. Interestingly, this study did not find a difference in support between conscious and non-conscious processes.

MOVING BEYOND LIBERTARIAN PATERNALISM

As the opening paragraphs of this chapter indicate, the debate about libertarian paternalism is somewhat fruitless. It has encouraged behavioural scientists to defend positions they should not need to. The position that can be adopted is that nudges should be preferred not because they maintain liberty, but because they are good public policies. Policy-makers may adopt them if they are authorised correctly, have evidence behind them, are evaluated properly, and where any potential negative effects are outweighed by the benefits, so long as individual rights are not violated. In this way, the justification of public policy remains within the classic utilitarian tradition of ensuring the happiness of the greatest number, subject to constraints on moral and rights grounds. Policies are needed because they improve welfare. In fact, in later writings Sunstein (2014a: 18) moves closer to this position rather than defending libertarian paternalism. Nudges are defended as a form of paternalism, but the aim is to make policies more accountable, democratic, and responsive at the same time. They can be better defended the more policy is transparent and democratically controlled. This is the essence of Schmidt's (2017) argument.

Such an argument is helped by the 'All tools are informational now' position of this book. If there were a clear choice between nudge policies and tool-based measures for all policy choices, then it might be easier to distinguish more clearly autonomy-enhancing nudges from authoritative commands. But, in fact, nudges are tied up with every kind of policy intervention, making it impossible to distinguish between a tax change and the nudge for example, because the nudge is embodied in how the message is communicated. There is no autonomy that is violated in a norm-based message, because it is impossible not to pay taxes. If the person does not pay, there are fines, all of which information is contained in both the nudge letter and a non-behavioural equivalent. What the behavioural science is doing is to make the initial communication more social and more effective as a message.

With public policy, there is a danger that the intervention will violate ethical constraints, much as a research project would (see John 2017a), so that policy-makers like academics have to check whether any harm has been caused, such as distress from having the policy, and whether this can be justified by the benefits generated or can be limited in some way in the delivery of the policy. As with university ethical guidelines, the moral argument is not that deception is necessarily wrong but that it may or may not be justified in a case. If there is no other way of doing the policy, then after the event measures to inform citizens should be in place. As Sunstein (2016) discusses, these situations may not always be needed, as it is possible to get results even when people are being told about being nudged (Loewenstein et al. 2015), though this study was with an online sample and needs more replication and extension. It still remains possible that telling the respondent will create reactance, where people resist messages. In this case, it might be ethically defensible not to convey the message.

Deception is an important problem and should be avoided, especially with nudges that work well when delivered without the knowledge of the participant (see Bovens 2009). A more general concern comes from manipulation, that people might be encouraged to do things they do not really want to do, which arises from the way the information is presented, even if just short of deception. After-the-event justification that it is in the respondents' interests is not a strong enough defence, and, as with other kinds of more controversial nudges, certain strong kinds of manipulation will be off limits as a nudge, or the nudge can be altered to make it less manipulative (see Wilkinson 2013). There are also special cases where people might be more vulnerable and make bad choices as a result of nudges, for example if a mentally impaired person chooses a default pension scheme when it is not in the person's interests to do so. Overall, it is important to bear in mind that nudges are different from each other. Contexts and populations vary, and this adjusts the moral arguments in play (Bovens 2009).

It could be possible to build in more autonomy to the nudge than a first design might envisage. It might involve more publicity about the nudge at the point of delivery or ensuring that all the facts conveyed in the nudge will improve welfare, for example a statement of what current income would be lost if a pension default were not reversed. The information could also say that some people prefer not to save for pensions because they value current pleasure so much. In addition nudges could go the extra mile in ensuring that their intentions are good for the long-run benefits of those who are nudged. In the view of many critics of public policy (e.g. Dobson 2011), nudges come across as depoliticised and rather technocratic: by building in more thinking about the public choices, and being aware of different stages and joins in the political process, a broader and more legitimate form of intervention could emerge.

The joining of ethical thinking about public policy to conventions in research governance comes about because of the use of trials. In research, trials are thought to have special ethical problems from getting people to act in ways they would not otherwise choose to do, which need justification. It is the same with public policies that involve changing direct contact with the citizens, which is not altered from some exogenous factor but because of the science and knowledge of the researcher and policy-maker. While policy-makers can assume that a form of ethical approval comes from political authorisation, that politicians are put there to implement public policies for which they are judged at a subsequent election, and that their actions are accountable in the public sphere, such as parliamentary committees, questions in the chamber, or the actions of the courts, in practice democratic accountability and scrutiny cannot extend to the bureaucrats and their decisions at such a detailed level; hence there is a need for some kind of ethical sign-off or the building of ethical thinking into public policy. In this way, some of the more extreme nudges, which might involve deceiving people or making them think they are doing better than they really are, say in an employment search, can be ruled out or modified as a result of ethical scrutiny.

It so happens that nudges are less likely rather than more likely to breach an ethical constraint, because of their gentleness, at least in general, and because they tend to go with the grain of human preferences. In choosing between compelling people to do something, punishing them if they do not do it, and a nudge, where people are encouraged to do something, the criterion is not just respect for freedom but non-coercive approaches being more likely to work in today's anti-authoritarian climate. People resent being told what to do, and they resist strong messages. They are more likely to be responsive to the state or public agency that nudges, because the approach implies a conversation with citizens rather than the state or agency stamping its authority over them. The listening and sensitive state is what this book is seeking to encourage.

CONCLUSION

The core argument in this chapter is that although there are important ethical issues to consider when carrying out behavioural public policies or nudges, which may even result in their modification or abandonment, there is no fundamental ethical objection that rules nudges out or prevents a sizeable number of them from being implemented. This simple claim is because nudges are public policies authorised by democratically elected governments that are subject to review. Those who introduce nudges are accountable just as any other policy-makers seeking to improve welfare. Ethical acceptability depends on how open and effective are the procedures for authorisation. Like public policies, nudges raise ethical issues of harm to people and need to ensure the right balance of trade-offs between objectives citizens care about, such as welfare on the one hand and equality, justice, and rights on the other. Nudges are in the mainstream. Because nudges are so closely linked to other tools of government, such as laws, fines, incentives and so on, it does not make sense to distinguish particular moral claims about using a nudge from those deriving from using another instrument. Issues around proportionality, fairness, responsiveness, and reasonableness appear just as much with laws and fines as they do with nudges, in that policy is more desirable if it accords with democratic values and is more likely to work in terms of getting compliance if these values influence the design of the policy instruments.

To the extent that there is a clear choice between a nudge and a more authoritative instrument of government, there is good reason to choose the nudge, because, as Sunstein (2017b) argues, it is less likely to cause reactance; in other words, nudges might be more effective as a result of being light-touch. They have been discovered as a policy partly as a result of the failure of traditionally applied tools of government (see John 2011). Some nudges (but not all of them) might enhance autonomy and can help guide citizens to make more autonomous choices in the longer term. These are the types of nudges that it would be best to approve of and to develop. In that sense, there could be a moral purpose behind nudging, but only if additional aspects to the intervention are introduced, in particular to the way individuals are guided. Nudges are not by necessity autonomy enhancing, but they can be. Nudges could be further developed to be more in line with the values of democracy. This project is the task of the remainder of the book.

8.   Nudge plus and how to get there

Previous chapters of this book have provided an extensive review of the development of behavioural public policy, largely with approval of the valued added of such a programme. There has been an acknowledgement of the ease with which ideas in behavioural economics have transferred into concrete policy proposals that sit well with the preferences of bureaucrats. These measures have been tested with randomised evaluations and then introduced into the standard operating procedures of agencies. The central parts of the book show the diffusion of these policies across fields of activity and jurisdictions, and the general welfare-enhancing benefits of such changes are in evidence. The criticisms of nudges, at least in a simple form that they do not work and offer no benefits, do not stand up. Moreover, there are relatively few special ethical constraints on the use of nudges, even though ethical constraints should not be waved away and are important considerations in the design of these policies.

Having shown the development of nudge, its benefits, and the lack of constraints on its use, the task now is to see if the policy agenda can be extended and expanded; whether there is greater potential for nudging, especially given the variation in the kinds that can be done, as there are a considerable number of choices about how such nudges are carried out and which ones are followed. The argument is that nudges can move more in a direction that involves some kind of reflection on the part of the individual, at least as an element of the nudge, or a process of reflection before or after a nudge has been delivered, ensuring that a nudge operates on the boundary of system 1 and system 2 thinking. When more reflective processes are engaged, the idea is that nudge gets closer to the ideal of democratic self-government, as a means for the state to help its citizens take back some control over their lives in the long run, which is part of the attractiveness of Sunstein's soft paternalism.

As well as expanding the scope of nudging, it is possible to alter the subject of the nudge, that is the person or organisation that gives the nudge, so that nudging is more inclusive and can address inequalities of political power. This inclusion involves more equality between the citizen and the state. It can be the basis for a more open conversation about public policy, which is based more on think and deliberative mechanisms. The argument is that a more extended and radical form of nudging could come about that builds on the strength of what has been achieved, which can challenge elites as well as be used by them.

THE THINK IN NUDGE

A core idea in behavioural sciences is system 1 or automatic processes: that humans act from unconscious mechanisms in their brains, which have biases or heuristics baked into them, so that individuals make many decisions, sometimes important ones, based on these intuitions, 'thinking fast' to use the language of Kahneman (2011). There may be many advantages to working in this way, in that it reduces the need for cognitive capacity, makes many choices unproblematic, and allows human beings to concentrate on things they want to think about, so that many actions, such as driving a car, doing the shopping, or even carrying out routine tasks at home like settling bills and doing housework, are routine and do not burden people with unnecessary choices. These shortcuts can be useful in making larger decisions if they remove a long set of calculations that would in any case have caused the individual to come to the same decision. If an individual is loyal to a political party that represents his or her interest and so long as the party does act in the interests of the individual, then what is the point of assessing the choices and reading all the party programmes if in the end the person is going to make the choice to vote for that party? Early work in political science recognised this, for example Downs (1957), who regarded heuristics as a way to economise on information searching, called 'rational ignorance'.

Big and important decisions may be made in the same way. But how do individuals know whether to let the automatic processes take hold or to stop to consider options, that is move to Kahneman's system 2 processes of slow thinking and more careful consideration? For example, house purchase, as any real estate agent knows, is highly automatic, with many decisions taking place in a matter of minutes as the potential purchaser walks round the property. This rapid decision-making can lead to poor decisions. It also means that purchasers are subject to manipulation by agents and disguising of the quality of the property by vendors. But a lot of purchases are done in communities known to the buyers, with say rows of terraces where the houses are quite similar, and the buyers typically know these areas and properties well, as they tend to move within the area in which they already live, so the final decision can be based on matters of taste about decor and small variations in design.

The level of risk may be reduced by the choice of a standard property. Perhaps individuals know about this risk, which explains the conservative nature of many moving choices. Moreover, regulators can be used to check up on details later on, and rules may allow a period of reflection afterward. But, of course, many decisions, as has been found in health, happen over a long period of time where the error is not detected or corrected. Some hasty decision-making causes people to buy poor financial products or household appliances. If people can avoid getting feedback on decisions they fear or regret, they do. There is hence a possibility of having the opportunity to rethink options but choosing not to. With political parties, supporters may stay loyal to their brand long after their party has changed its policies to please new types of voters. Rather than pursuing rational ignorance, people need to keep half an eye on information flows and update their views from time to time.

Rather than impose their own ideas or try to reason with people, behavioural scientists find that it makes sense to take advantage of automatic processes to design proposals that move people away from their own automatic processes or those used by the private sector. They combat foe with foe in effect. The nudges that work at an automatic level can correct for errors without the citizen being really aware of them. As the initiatives in this book have shown, there are a number of advantages of taking this approach when there is discretion in any case over the delivery of policies. These initiatives can have large effects. But there are some limitations, as Chapter 6 indicates. One is that the changes may be focused on the minority of people who are willing to change their behaviour. The effects may diminish over time. The approach concentrates on small behaviour changes, whereas dealing with a large public problem, such as the environment, needs sustained and greater behaviour change over a range of issues. There is also the problem of the lack of consent of the citizens to those changes, which can cause the problem that if they do not agree with the objectives of the change they may react negatively from reactance if they find out. However, it may be the case that it is easy to apply this approach at the early stage of the behavioural agenda when the choices are ones that no one would disagree with and individuals would not mind. More complex behaviour changes might involve making more fundamental changes where it might not seem obvious to individuals and it could take time for them to realise it is in their long-term interests to change their behaviour.

The way out of the limitation is to say that all the nudges that have been carried out can be banked as good pieces of public policy, but also there is a case for reviewing where the agenda is right now, and to say that an opportunity exists to move it toward a different kind of nudging that is more inclusive and based more on self-control. But policy-makers should be cautious in considering more deliberative ways of involving citizens in public policy, which might sound a surprise given the way this argument is proceeding. But there are lessons from the fate of such initiatives in deliberative public policy.

The main argument for a more deliberative approach derives from the idea that citizens can shift their preferences if they debate about a policy initiative with more time, access to expert information, and appropriate facilitation (Dryzek 2000). This idea can be built into the design of many institutions as a form of democratic innovation (Smith 2009) beyond citizens' juries and deliberative polling (e.g. Fiskin 1995) favoured in much of the pioneering work on deliberation. In particular, a more deliberative approach can be incorporated into public policy, through providing genuine citizen input into decision-making, before major decisions are made rather than afterwards just to legitimate them or as meaningless consultation. In the design and also the delivery and implementation of public policies, citizen input can guide public decisions, which feeds into more responsive and efficient policies. This benefit has been illustrated in case studies of citizen initiatives, such as participatory budgeting in Porto Allegre or policing in Chicago (Fung 2006). From the public policy perspective, it is not a case of policies emerging top down, but being discussed and owned by the people involved. As a result of ownership, policy outcomes improve, partly from public bureaucracies working more efficiently and responsively, but also because citizens are cooperating in acts of collective endeavour. It is not hard to see this as a form of behaviour change policy whereby behaviours are modified as a result of what happens in the policy process. Behaviour change can happen individually as a form of response to public policies and decisions taken in the public realm, and it can be a form of collective action whereby people overcome the obstacles to behaving in more beneficial ways for society as a whole.

When the deliberative project has a particular policy focus it can be compared to the nudging as described in this book. This was the idea behind *Nudge, Nudge, Think, Think* (John et al. 2011), a book based on collaborative research that tested the efficacy of nudge as opposed to think strategies, using trials as the main method of evaluation. What was found was that most of the nudge policies worked in the sense of delivering changes in behaviour, with reasonable effect sizes given the mild nature of the interventions, but it was much harder to conclude that many of the think policies were as effective. In one case the think strategy was good at getting the citizens to consider behaviour change. The agency responded to their complaints by asking them to consider volunteering, but the organisation found it hard to respond with activities for the citizens to participate in. The citizens were mobilised to turn from complainers into deliberators, but the infrastructure and support were not there to allow them to do so.

Another experiment tested whether a nudge or a think would be more effective in getting students to consider donating their organs in the event of their death, comparing the nudge (nudging information), a think (a discussion), and a placebo. The nudge worked the best and then the placebo, but the think did much worse than the placebo. Thinking and debating do not necessarily lead to the desired policy outcome, and nudging might be the best choice in many circumstances. But maybe it was good that human subjects did not conform to what was expected of them – they were entitled to consider the policy area in their own way, so they decided that donations were not for them, having thought about the problem. How can any democrat argue against this kind of reasoning on the part of citizens? Otherwise thinking would only be fine if it came up with the right decision from the state's point of view. The example also illustrates some of the costs of a deliberative approach to public policy in that it is not usually possible to have the space to discuss things fully, as in citizens' juries or even budget discussions or policy implementation. Could such small thinks really be a recipe for general policy advocacy? It is hard to get citizens to deliberate, as was found in the online scaling-up exercise in *Nudge, Nudge, Think, Think* (John et al. 2011), where few engaged in this way, preferring to listen (or lurk) rather than engage (see also Smith et al. 2013). It was hardly surprising there were modest effects in this experiment. This limitation goes back to the conventional criticisms of non-representative democracy mechanisms that they place a high burden on citizens in terms of their time and capacity to process large amounts of information. Partly as a result, they tend to attract a minority non-representative sample of the population, including those who are available to be manipulated, and the subset of people who do change their behaviour is very small. The online deliberation reported in Smith et al. (2013) still only attracted a minority of the citizens, who themselves were self-selected respondents in the polling company's online survey bank. These were further self-selected into those who agreed to participate and did not drop out. But if deliberation does not easily scale up, the question is whether nudges, which can reach everyone, can include a deliberative and thinking element, ensuring that all affected do this to a certain extent rather than self-select. Can nudges do justice to the complexity of the policy choice under consideration?

MORE OPEN NUDGES: NUDGE PLUS

In order to move beyond the dichotomy between nudging and thinking, it is important to return again to the important distinction between system 1 and system 2 thinking. None of the proponents says there is a hard-and-fast distinction. It is true that different parts of the brain are involved and there is secure knowledge in neuroscience behind these findings. But it is not possible to say that automatic processes are only engaged with nudges and that other parts of the brain are not working to a small degree. Even in the most impulsive moment most people have an awareness of the choices they face, or hold back just for a second. Going back to that house-buying decision, which is sometimes made at the viewing, there is often a moment in the car or on the bus on the way back home when the person is struck by the importance of the decision made and may feel a sense of regret , which is again an automatic response, but is based on an awareness of the choice and can lead to a reconsideration of the decision down the line. The example is a reminder that the time period for the operation of a nudge can be long, which might include a rash decision, reflection, and then another change of course (which justifies the creation of choice architectures that allow for changes in decisions or cooling-off periods). Another example might be an unrealistic diet that is not kept to, but the person thinks of a more reasonable way to reach the goal of achieving weight loss in the long term. The thought process is that someone can understand a breach of the diet for special occasions or treats, but the idea is that the individual finds a sustainable strategy over the long term which involves steering, responding to situations, and knowing her or his limitations and strengths.

The other factor to bear in mind is that nudges often require prior understanding, which implies a degree of cognitive engagement and the ability to understand the causal links. In behavioural science, for example, it has been shown that conveying the costs of attendance or carrying out an action for the public purse has positive effects. Hallsworth et al. (2015) randomised SMS messages to outpatients in the NHS with a treatment message that indicated the costs of missing an appointment and which led to fewer people missing their appointments. It could be that this is purely automatic, activating a norm of attendance. But it is more complex than this. What is happening is that patients are being asked to think about the consequences of their decisions. It is not a simple nudge based on an automatic response, at least not in full, but requires the respondent to understand the argument that missed appointments cost money and that turning up helps the public service. This kind of act cannot be seen as purely system 1 even if system 1 needs to be in play.

In a more sophisticated application of this kind of treatment, John and Blume (2017) sought to nudge holders of blue badges, which allow disabled people to park their cars in designated places so it is easier for them to get to shops and public facilities, to renew online, which is much cheaper for the local authority that issues the badges. The researchers tested a nudge in a reminder letter that said that the public authority would save money if people renewed online, which worked in generating considerable savings for the authority. The implication of the successful message is that recipients understood the argument that was being made and then believed the council would spend the saved resources on public services. For the intervention to work, there had to be trust in the local elected public authority not to waste the money, which is not easily assumed in this age of declining faith in politics and those in public life.

Even more standard nudges require some thought on the part of the respondent, as they are often seeking to convey an action in a complex public policy system. The humble nudge 'Nine out of ten people have already paid their taxes' requires the respondent to understand what this phrase means. As well as following the norm, which might be automatic, the taxpayers might also think about the likelihood of being caught and whether paying up rectifies this risk, which requires a conception about how payment systems work.

Nudges to change health behaviour often require that the people in the trial have gone through a thought process about how the desired actions will affect them, as otherwise the interventions would not have a chance of working. Consider commitment devices (Thaler and Shefrin 1981). These are concrete and public commitments people make or are encouraged to make to do an action so as to commit themselves to it. Although the nudge operates through the psychological sense of commitment and not wanting to go back on something for fear of feeling guilty, in fact entering into a commitment device requires some degree of thought and understanding of what a commitment device is in the first place. In many ways, communicating this set of understandings is the only way to ensure a successful nudge. Imagine people being duped into accepting a commitment device. It is unlikely that this device would have any worth, because the people would not really understand it. Even if they did, they might say they did not really want to do it. A lot of mental ground needs to be covered before some nudges can work. A nudge also works much better when the respondent thinks about it. There is quite a bit of evidence that commitment devices work, such as in health (Savani 2017). But the focus in the debate is how such devices work once they have been agreed to (the doer) rather than the decision to take on a commit-ment device in the first place (the planner). The latter involves thought and reflection on the part of the individual, which is part of the programme of nudge plus that is the core argument of *How Far to Nudge?*

Consider the placement of healthy options next to the tills in cafeterias. The automatic nudge works like this: people are stimulated to buy chocolate and sweets, as they are near the till. They have made their main food choices and are waiting to pay. Their eyes focus on the products conveniently placed at eye level. The love of chocolate and sweet things plays a role in that the consumer almost subconsciously places the bar on the tray. It gets paid for and eaten pleasurably later on. Now consider the placement of fruit near the checkout. Unless someone has a craving for fruit, then that person will see the fruit but will not be prompted in the same way. It works rather differently. The person sees the fruit and then has to think along the following lines: 'Well, have I had enough fruit and vegetables today, my five portions, so it is OK not to buy more fruit?' Or the person could say: 'No, I had better have some fruit, as I only had cereal this morning.' The person feels a lot better from having fulfilled a moral commitment, which is consciously acted upon, even though the person was nudged when waiting to pay for the food. There is no benefit, especially in the long term, in people half-accidentally putting fruit on their trays. They will probably leave the fruit behind when they come to stack the tray.

Another example of these thought-provoking nudges is the work on aspirations to motivate people to make better choices, such as to go to university. The choice to go to university often is not based on ability, but on students feeling they need to go and leave their families and friends to advance their careers and life chances. Experimental research shows that people can be influenced by communications, especially from someone they admire, to make the choice to attend university. One example is a letter to the student from someone at the university (Sanders et al. 2017). Silva et al. (2016) found that role models giving talks to students works too. What is going on with these interventions? It is not the classic prompt of the subconscious nudge. Students need to understand and think about the message. They need to think through a set of linkages, which involves the idea that someone like them might attend university or go on to better employment.

One of the key ideas in Kahneman (2011) is that not only are system 1 and system 2 separate, but they closely relate to each other. The active self guides more automatic actions and lays in place ways in which these automatic actions can work as if the more thinking self were in charge.

Service and Gallagher (2017) explore the idea of scaffolding in their book *Think Small*, the idea that supporting structures are needed to help individuals achieve their goals, which may be several, and where nudgers should be focused when trying to develop the goals in the first place. These are what they call 'self-nudges', and include focusing on choosing the appropriate goal, focusing on a single objective, and breaking it down to manageable steps. Service and Gallagher (2017) use examples from the practical application of behavioural insights, such as with welfare-to-work, to make their case. The result should be self-sustaining. But what they show is not the classic nudges where an automatic behaviour is stimulated, but where individuals take control of their own nudges. The key word in the book's title is 'think', of course!

Another application is where nudges are made more personal or personalised to appeal to the individual. An example is including the person's name as part of a request to settle court fines (Haynes et al. 2013). This again can be regarded cynically as a ploy to make citizens think that someone is taking a personal interest but in fact could be a way to stimulate people's interest and engagement with the problem, in that someone in officialdom is taking an interest in them: if someone takes an interest, they take more of an interest in themselves, which may involve some reflection and conscious thought.

A recent evaluation of crime re-education policies for poor youth in Chicago (Heller et al. 2017), using evidence from three randomised controlled trials, showed that the Becoming a Man (BAM) programme developed by the Chicago non-profit Youth Guidance reduced total arrests during the intervention period by 28–35 per cent, reduced violent-crime arrests by 45–50 per cent, improved school engagement, increased graduation rates by 12–19 per cent and reduced readmission rates to a correctional facility by 21 per cent. Heller et al. (2017) tested whether people in the programme show more slow thinking by playing a game, which they do. They conclude that they have 'suggestive support for the hypothesis that the programs work by helping youth slow down and reflect on whether their automatic thoughts and behaviours are well suited to the situation they are in, or whether the situation could be construed differently' (Heller et al. 2017: 2). Recent work shows the influence of therapy-based interventions on social outcomes. Blattman et al. (2017) tested whether providing cognitive behavioural therapy (CBT) would improve outcomes, crime, and violence for unemployed youth in Liberia, which they found to have strong effects. There has been a more general interest in using ideas in CBT as a tool to increase awareness of people's own behaviour changes, influencing initiatives such as mindfulness, which can be taught and conveyed so as to achieve behaviour change, and can even be targeted to policy-makers (see Lilley et al. 2014). What is interesting from the nudge plus perspective is the extent to which the behaviour changes come from measures that stimulate reflection and awareness.

In recent years, there has been a lot of focus on what characteristics might be associated with long-term behaviour change, or self- and societal benefiting behaviours. Is it possible to engage in a programme of achieving long-term goals? In the view of psychologists like Duckworth et al. (2007), it requires the development of orientations akin to determination and playing for the long term, what they call 'grit'. In studies of health it requires having a particular mind-set to engage in change (Burd 2016). Though some of these characteristics might derive from genes or family context, the message from advocates of grit is that individuals can consciously work at improving them. This activity must involve some thinking and reflection on the part of individuals, even if the later actions might follow more automatically. That is because the main factor beyond successful behaviour change is effective motivation (see Michie et al. 2011), and this underlying feature can only be tackled by some degree of reflection and consideration on the part of individuals.

The grit idea sounds tautological (it describes the success rather than the nudge, and grit describes people who are successful, not how they got there). There is little evidence for it in experimental evaluations (e.g. Heller et al. 2017), and it does not correlate with outcomes, for example in education (Rimfeld et al. 2016). But it does make sense that capabilities can be cultivated. To get there, they may need a 'boost', which is a term that has recently appeared in work on nudging (Grüne-Yanoff and Hertwig 2016).

The boost argument works in many medical situations where people need capacity to make decisions. In the past, doctors used to dispense their decisions from on high for grateful patients to receive. Now, in the days of consumer sovereignty, patients are given choices between alternative courses of action, say different treatments. These choices require some understanding of the statistics, and it is easy to make simple mistakes. This problem was identified in Kahneman and Tversky's research (e.g. Kahneman et al. 1982), which affects elite decision-makers like doctors too. From a boost perspective, the question is whether there are things that can increase capacity, or nudges that encourage people to exercise choices with better knowledge of the consequences. At the same time, it is important to realise it is not possible to offer an introductory lesson on probability. What people need is nudges to help them to make better choices but still based on their own reasoning. An example Hertwig (2017) gives is the information about the risk of different treatments expressed as natural frequencies rather than in conditional probabilities, so avoiding a need to understand Bayesian statistics. This training strategy has proved effective (Sedlmeier and Gigerenzer 2001). Other examples include rules of thumb to interpret financial investment decisions for retirement, or simple rules to follow for a diet. In Hertwig's (2017) words, 'The goal of boosts is to make it easier for people to exercise their own agency in making choices.' The proposals help get over the paternalist problem as well as make choices better because they put the individual more in control rather than being pushed along by a discrete nudge.

The benefit from thinking more broadly is that a greater number of behaviours can be altered. In the above examples, the increase is over time, so actions are repeated. There could be expansion across the range of actions, what is called 'behavioural spillover', whereby a new behaviour in one sphere causes behaviour change in another (Dolan and Galizzi 2015). Part of the reason for this phenomenon is that 'we may derive satisfaction not just from tangible behavioral outcomes, but also from the accumulation of signals and beliefs about our own identities' (Dolan and Galizzi 2015: 4). The chances of behavioural spillovers are much greater if individuals have shifted their approach to life so that a change in one area, for example improving diet, is complemented by a change in another, such as taking exercise, drinking less, or recycling more, taking on the attributes of good citizens. Nudges that target the motivation of citizens or appeal to their identity have more potency. They work better when consciously thought about, which can help reverse some tendencies for negative spillover, such as coasting after carrying out a good deed.

This kind of nudging works better if there is a long-term relationship between the individual and the public agency. Consider the process of giving feedback, for example, on the performance of someone doing the action, such as giving people a smiley if residents on their street have recycled their waste more than the average for the area (John et al. 2011). Here there are stages to the action, not just a one-off nudge. The start is the state before the nudge, then the nudge to change behaviour, then the feedback and then the change in behaviour as a result of the feedback. All of this may seem to be capable of being manipulated, but in fact the stages show how the thoughts of the nudged and the nudger need to be synchronised. Most of all, to respond to the feedback the citizen needs to understand what is going on: that the objective is good, that it makes sense to respond, that keeping up with others as part of the agenda for change is desirable, and that being reminded is to be part of the conversation. It would be even better if the citizens, having changed their behaviours, got a thank-you message from the authority. Indeed, research on the impact of thanking someone for voting indicates it also has the benefit of encouraging further participation at a subsequent election (Panagopoulos 2011).

The goal of nudging must be some long-term change to which the individual has given some thought. The commitment is a way of grounding the new form of behaviour. There is a need to put into place a self-equilibrating system so things happen automatically and are self-sustaining. The goal is a rule-based system which is not enforced, rather as with the *Highway Code*, which is really about social cooperation, with the state only as a back-up when behaviours go badly awry.

In some ways, this argument is an extension of the original Thaler and Sunstein (2008) claim that people would not mind being nudged if they had the chance to think about it. It is a small extra step to believing that the nudge operates well on the basis of previous thought, which is then acted upon. There will be some reflection, which soon becomes embedded in automatic processes. Nobody wants to be permanently thinking about public policy as in the deliberative ideal, but people want to be autonomous in the way they respond to nudges. The idea is that a combination of nudging and thinking can help the creation of an automated and self-regulating system whereby people get to their goals and where there is a synergy between social and individual aims. Rather than nudges only being acceptable and practicable if people think about them when being influenced in their behaviour, people can consider and reflect on them, even if they do this only very briefly, before or after the nudge or both. The actual nudge can be automatically responded to, but individuals benefit from prior or subsequent thought about the context and justification of the interventions. This argument, in Mols et al.'s (2015) view, is more psychologically plausible and in line with how long-term behaviour change comes about: 'enduring behaviour change involves an identity-change process whereby people proactively choose to engage in behaviour that is perceived as identity-consistent and therefore seen as "the right thing to do"' (Mols et al. 2015: 82–83). They argue that nudges will be more effective if they key into people's social identity. Whether the end result is automatic and non-conscious behaviour matters less. It is more convenient and self-sustained if people do not always think about the choices. It is merely that their current choices have been considered and understood at some point.

People can be affected by the environment within which choices are made and whereby people may seize effective opportunities. In this sense, the automatic processes can affect how people think. It is possible to redesign buildings so that people interact rather more, and stand rather than sit, which increases well-being and the ability to make decisions (Engelen et al. 2016). A systematic review of workplace reorganisations (Bambra et al. 2007) stresses the importance of control in the workplace for well-being and argues for more participation.

In many ways, these nudges, which are about public goods and general public policy outcomes, are different to the private sector nudges which are about clicking on some part of a website, or ensuring customers are 'hot' when making a purchasing decision, or showing how many rooms are left on a hotel booking website and how many people are currently watching them. Often there is much more involved with the action than individualised purchasing decisions. There are complex public policy issues where some awareness of the issues and of the behaviour is needed as the baseline for the nudge to work, as people know this is not a simple request. Then there is the communication about the public nature of the goods being provided in that the nudge is really one part of a larger set of actions about public provision.

In this sense, no one should be surprised by the finding that most nudges are not carried out in secret, but are authorised publicly and appear on the website of the Behavioural Insights Team or another nudging organisation. It is easy to find out what the state is doing to individuals. There is even publicity about those nudges that find their way into the press and other forms of media. This is not just some act of organisational survival; it is actually an important part of nudging. It is all part of the conversation, which need not happen all in one go, but is iterative and a long-term project of better communication between the government and citizens. The result is implied consent to behavioural public policy, which is backed up by detailed survey evidence. Sunstein (2016) shows that citizens approve of nudges when they learn about them so long as these interventions are consistent with their long-term objectives. If the research by Loewenstein et al. (2015) is a full guide, and to an extent it is preliminary, nudgers should be encouraged that telling people about nudges does not undermine support for them. Moreover, Bruns et al. (2016) find that transparency does not reduce the effectiveness of nudges. People do not display reactance when they find out.

The argument is that nudges already contain a thinking component, even if understated, which means that the next generation of nudges could expand this aspect. This wider range for nudge falls short of the think argued for in John et al. (2011), but is more feasible than, and an improvement on, the classic nudges. As a result, the research programme is an expansion or enhancement of the nudging programme, which John and Stoker (2017) call 'nudge plus'.

INCREASING THE RANGE OF SUBJECTS AND OBJECTS WITH NUDGE

If the previous section was about focusing on and selecting nudges that have a deliberative and reflective component, this section is about increasing the range of nudges to different kinds of people or organisations so they can be both nudgers and nudged. The current manifestation of nudge has been focused often on a central government unit that has been set up in the centre of government with the authority of the prime minister or leading figures. The nudges are as a result top down, as is the operation of a nudge unit, which appears to be a strong centre using the insights of behaviour change to effect change. In fact, as Chapter 5 shows, this image is a false one, in that the central units did not have much power and relied on persuading and enthusing others in the bureaucracy to engage in behaviour change, generally in pilot or demonstration projects. The agenda relied on diffusing ideas across the complex and myriad agencies of the state. Nudges need to be owned by an agency and do not usually work in a top-down way. They rely on enthusiasm and embedding behaviour change into bureaucracies and for agencies to adopt the ideas in a decentralised way. Entrepreneurs flourish in this environment, and they do not work well with strong control procedures. Pluralist nudges help avoid organisational mistakes and limit the effects of hierarchy. They ensure a responsible bureaucracy with multiple sources of information, and provide correction and control.

It is relatively easy to extend this model of diffusion to outside central government, which reflects the pattern of adoption of behaviour change. Of course, any agency can use behaviour change ideas, especially as such ideas work well in implementation processes, which are myriad across the complex web of government and agencies. Such a process was identified by Thaler and Sunstein: 'Workplaces, corporate boards, universities, religious organizations, clubs, and even families might be able to use, and to benefit from, small exercises in libertarian paternalism' (Thaler and Sunstein 2008: 252). It is possible to see the extension of nudge to local government and its agencies. The voluntary sector is a useful conduit for nudges, which are already being used to reach clients and to market charitable acts. There is no reason not to include community and citizen groups as part of the diffusion, with the main constraint being the capacity of small organisations to introduce nudges and to evaluate them with trials. Trials can diffuse to the private sector, of course, and this can be part of the intellectual climate of change, but raises ethical issues about using nudges for private means. The same can be said for the consultancies and private organisations that sell nudges to the public and private sector, with the danger that the provision of nudges becomes a commercial activity and reduces the chance that a more open and feedback-orientated version of nudge can prevail. The changes highlighted so far may challenge standard models of public administration based on relationships between politicians and bureaucrats, and between politicians/bureaucrats and citizens. This connects to a wider movement and set of theorising about a more decentralised and citizen-centred form of public management. Behavioural public policy resonates with such changes, and the rest of this chapter explores the linkages, possibilities for reform, and what model of bureaucracy and politics follows from behavioural policy.

CONTROLLING ELITES WITH NUDGES

Even with the decentralisation to smaller organisations, the relationship between governments and citizens or organisations or client groups remains the same: leaders and bureaucrats designing nudges to effect change on citizens. The final move in the argument is to consider whether nudges can be expanded to a more general political tool, which can be used by citizens as well as those in government. The starting point of the argument is that nudging rests on a belief that rational policy-makers use knowledge to design policies to correct the biases of citizens. Of course, the policy proceeds from the setting of objectives and then creating the means to achieve those objectives (using evidence), at least in formal terms (see John 2013b), but deviation from rational decision-making is common wisdom among policy scholars, as was reviewed in Chapters 1 and 3. Even though there are procedures in place to ensure the weighing of options, and options analysis to help decision-making, in the end gut feeling, intuition and emotion play their role in the selection of policies and even in monitoring implementation processes. Brest (2013) reviews the policy-making literature and identifies a number of common behavioural errors that policy-makers make: hindsight bias, anchoring, confirmation bias, overweighing slender evidence sources, poor interpretation of statistical evidence, availability bias, affect heuristic (using emotion to make decisions), psychic numbing (from overexposure to statistical evidence), overconfidence, stereotyping, choice overload, loss aversion, myopia, use of social proofs, and classic groupthink, which are quite resistant to what he calls 'de-biasing', removing those biases and improving the evidence base of decision-makers. In short, the same biases affect policy-makers as citizens.

The large literature on policy failures and successes is a tribute to the non-rational factors in the policy process, whereby policy-makers often ignore evidence in favour of their own gut feelings or just their lust for power and fame (Dunleavy 1995; McConnell 2010; King and Crewe 2013). The experiment by Loewen et al. (2014) is very instructive. The researchers recruited politicians to do an experiment based on the famous one carried out by Kahneman et al. (1982), the Asian disease test, to see if their reasoning was different to that of non-politicians considering the same problem. This is also a reminder that the original work of behavioural economists, such as Tversky and Kahneman (1981), was directed to elites and small groups (such as statisticians or pilots) rather than to the population at large. The experiment asks people to respond to the following scenario: 'An exotic disease is coming, and it'll kill 600 people. You have two options. Choose the first, and 400 people will die. Choose the second, and you take a risk: There's a two-thirds chance that everyone will die.' When you change the frame to a third chance of saving everyone there is movement upwards, as people are not avoiding the negative frame. When the Asian disease question was put to 154 Belgian, Canadian, and Israeli members of parliament, they behaved just as Kahneman et al. (1982) said, with no difference from the citizens, who may have done better than the politicians (who fear negative outcomes). The question is whether these biases are permanent features of decision-making, so creating persistent errors in the policy-making process, or whether there is scope for policy-makers to correct their mistakes. In a very pessimistic point of view, politicians appear to repeat errors, which is the implication of King and Crewe's (2013) book on policy fiascos.

But other parts of this literature are more optimistic, such as McConnell (2010) and Bovens et al. (2001), who look for the conditions for success in public policies. So, given biases, how can policy-makers correct their errors? A key form of correction comes from communications from citizens, who can feed back to politicians to show how well they are doing. These kinds of communication are in any case usually part of an intelligence strategy in the field of policy implementation, or act as a fire alarm to overcome the limits of the principal–agent relationship. But the problem is that, if the information is being communicated in a way that assumes a rational agent is receiving it, there is a danger that the information may overload, or the individual might not receive the information or see it as important. The politician in this respect is no different to the citizen who gets the outcome of a public information campaign. The result might be a lack of concentration and sense of overload, and no indication that the information is important.

There is an example of how this happens in practice. Richardson and John (2012) conducted an experiment to see whether a better-argued lobby would get more of a response than a worse-argued one. They recruited lobby groups to make a case for a policy change, and got them to send a councillor, on the basis of random allocation, either a well-worded letter or one that used poorer and less coherent arguments. The result of the experiment was that there was no difference in responses to the letters: the intervention made no difference to the response rate. The conclusion to draw from this experiment is that communications from citizens or citizen groups need to use some of the behavioural techniques to ensure politicians take notice and correct their errors. There is not much sense in using rational techniques to correct biases which are entrenched. Just as with nudging, it is better to confront bias with bias. There might be normative and practical reasons why citizens would not even want their leaders to be rational calculators, but would prefer them to have the same human emotions as they do themselves and to react in a human way to crises and problems. In the television series *Star Trek*, Spock with his rational facilities and willing-ness to use them was a useful and essential part of the crew, but many of the episodes showed the limitations of this kind of thinking. In contrast, the verve of the more impulsive Kirk won the day in the end. Aside from media convention, much of this appeal is about leadership, which is about politicians being human. If there is negativity bias among elites, it might come from understanding of the negativity bias of citizens. The biases of the two are equivalent. But communication between the two could be a form of correction, ensuring that politicians are emotional when they need to be and more rational when that is better. Or it could be that communicating and acting on the biases where appropriate would be a better form of decision-making, where both governing and governed realise the importance of heuristics, a sort of conscious bias. Gigerenzer and Brighton (2009) refer to 'homo heuristicus', who may be able to handle decisions in a more efficient way than someone with the infor-mation overload implied by the rational model: 'a biased mind can handle uncertainty more efficiently and robustly than an unbiased mind relying on more resource-intensive and general-purpose processing strat-egies' (Gigerenzer and Brighton 2009: 109). This factor is why program-mers insert heuristics into artificial intelligence systems to make them smart. But rather than having elites working on their own, it could be argued that heuristics might be more successful if done in communi-cation between elites and non-elites. It can encourage both to reflect on new information brought by the other rather than just being nudged.

However, work on judgement and decision-making indicates that heuristics perform well but not significantly differently from other decision-making aids (Chater et al. 2003).

There is a considerable amount of evidence from what are called 'elite experiments' that politicians and bureaucrats do take notice of behavioural cues. It is possible to randomise these communications, in what are called 'experiments on institutions' (Grose 2014). For example, Grose (2010) randomised the legislators of a state to receive a message saying they were being observed by an outside group. This message led to increased attendance at committees. Nyhan and Reifler (2015) carried out an experiment which fact-checked legislators in nine US states.

It might reasonably be thought that the inequality of resources will continue in the age of behavioural sciences. The advantages of nudge accrue to those who have power and access to these resources. They can use the techniques of behavioural sciences to control citizens rather than vice versa, which would fit the pattern of the development of the science so far. But this use of nudge does not reflect the development of modern politics, which has been transformed by the expansion of information in recent years, and in particular the sharing of information across citizens and a wide range of groups. The expansion of the internet and the use of social media mean that people are connected in real time and that they have the ability to contribute content with maximum impact at next to zero costs. This facility increases the chances of political participation and creates large swings in movements and ideas that challenge political elites (Margetts et al. 2016), which has put those in government on the back foot in many cases, though of course they can adapt. The rise of a more fast-moving and turbulent politics will necessitate the use of the ideas of behavioural sciences, both by citizens seeking policy change and by politicians changing their courses of action in response. Because of much of internet politics being done so quickly and where communications between people can be responded to in real time, in particular where the internet is able to communicate social information, such as how many other people are carrying out an activity (social norms), then behaviourally coded information works very well on the internet and can be used by groups and citizens for any purpose. Social media politics then provides an arena within which behavioural nudges can thrive and be highly influential. Can this readiness to use social media be harnessed in a more responsive form of politics, which leads to correction, or does it imply that the already manifest tendency to bias that already exists will become exaggerated and maybe there will even be dangers to security and effective policy-making?

The danger with the reliance on citizen nudges or nudges from lower-level organisations is that there may be an inequality of power, which is only partly rectified by the dispersion of power from social media, as it may be the case that more powerful organisations are more skilful in using nudges. The other main disadvantage is that there is the possibility of evidence and expert correction in government nudges, no matter how cognitively bounded the decision-makers are, but such correction might not exist with citizen nudges. Lack of evidence, together with emotions, might actually bias the policy process even more than it does currently without them. Dependence on heuristics and short-term biases might foster anti-politics just as much as technocratic and expert policies do currently.

CONCLUSION

This chapter has sought to move the argument of the book beyond a review of existing evidence and research about the development of behavioural public policy to a consideration of where the research and policy agenda might go. It started from the difference between nudges for public policy concerns and nudges done for commercial advantage, as the former need citizens to be aware, to a degree, of complex linkages and citizen roles. It has been argued that public policy nudges are rarely purely system 1, that is just automatic, though some are. They usually involve some understanding of the objective of the nudge, which may involve some reflection, to ensure the nudge can work. Even where a nudge is unconsciously acted on, it is in fact based on a set of understandings and arguments that have already been established by the citizen. The effectiveness of intervention for diet and more exercise, for example, relies on the respondents being aware of the evidence and arguments about behaviour change, which ironically might have been conveyed by prior information campaigns so derided by nudge experts. Then the nudge might provoke some reflection after the event. The chapter gives some examples of these kinds of nudges and suggests nudge plus is an important area for expansion of behavioural public policy so as to incorporate some reflective component or element. The argument is that an enhanced nudge is much more desirable than full-on deliberation, which takes up too much time, assumes too much capacity, and only selects a minority of the population. As part of this process, government may seek to increase people's capacity to make choices, the 'boost' in Hertwig's (2017) terminology.

The expansion of nudge needs to go beyond the activities of centrally sponsored units, and should be used much more by decentralised organisations. At the heart of nudge is a more responsive form of decision-making, one that is more agile and attuned to where citizens are at cognitively. It can be used by anyone to promote the aims of other organisations or people, thereby helping rectify the inequalities of power and information between groups. There is the possibility of expansion downwards to lower-level organisations and to citizens themselves, to use the science for the ends of controlling decision-makers as well. The use of science that takes account of bias can be a more effective way of communicating with decision-makers, because the decision-makers suffer from bias too. They may not have enough time and mental capacity to respond to more informed communications.

9. Assessing behavioural public policy

The aim of this chapter is to come to an overall assessment about the potential for nudges. What is the full range of their application and the likelihood of their continuing success? The idea is to use the argument and evidence presented so far in this book to come to an appreciation about the current and future scope of nudging, which could be just using it in a minimal way, mainly about improving communications and transactions, or extending right up to the maximum possible use. The latter position is close to the argument of Chapter 8 with its advocacy of a decentralised nudge plus. If the intellectual device of a continuum of possible nudges is accepted, ranging between minimal and maximal, then the question is where to place preferences for actual policies and practices on it. Readers, given the extent to which they agree or disagree with the arguments made in previous chapters, may wish to place themselves on this scale and so answer the question of the book – How far to nudge? – themselves. Overall, there is a need to stand back and take on board the criticisms of nudge, as well as fully respond to the ethical challenges, paying attention to the debate about limitations and constraints introduced in Chapters 6 and 7. These cautionary considerations should not be lost in the enthusiasm for next-generation interventions.

In deciding how far to nudge, one option need not have serious consideration, which is the case for not nudging at all, which regards the use of behavioural economics as fundamentally negative when deployed by policy-makers, voluntary groups, and citizens. To come to such a pessimistic view, readers would need to have complete faith in the model of rational decision-making and simply want more information for citizens, with more effective applications of incentives and sanctions, in just the way Becker (1968) argued for, which is consistent with autonomy and transparency. Given common knowledge about human cognitions, a simple version of this model cannot apply: policy-makers need to take some account of citizen biases in order to achieve their objectives. It is possible to use some of the tools of rational action, modified in some way, to apply behavioural economics in ways that optimise behaviours, but this is a different position from not using the insights of behavioural economics.

The other argument for not using the science of behaviour change, which emerged in Chapter 6 on the criticisms of nudge, is that it represents an unacceptable loss of autonomy because it embodies forces in society and the economy that limit the freedom of individuals to make their own choices. The science of behaviour change offers to policy-makers a further means to reduce individual autonomy and gives them a more comprehensive set of tools with which to exercise power over citizens. It ensures the passivity of citizens in deciding matters of importance to them. Moreover, it depoliticises much of public policy into a set of technical questions rather than focusing on societal values and power relations, which affect the formulation and implementation of public policy. It further hands power to the experts and professionals. In this view, it is no surprise then that citizens are currently disengaged from politics and keen to follow a populist or radical agenda when taken advantage of in this way.

The anti-technical argument, however, is hard to sustain given how much is still up for choice by today's citizens and the openness of much behavioural public policy. To hold such a position, it needs to be assumed that powerful forces in society always control government and politics, limiting the autonomy of citizens. If this view is accepted, by definition any policy that comes from government is bound to have particular ideologies of control built into it. Democracy then becomes a sham. But even critical work on behaviour change holds back from this position whilst at the same time offering criticisms of the policies on offer.

If these two extreme positions – full rational action and ideological public policy – are rejected or at least limited as critiques, as it is sensible to do, then the question concerns the extent of the usage of behavioural techniques and assessing their full potential, which is affected by how long these innovations are going to last and whether they can bed down as permanent tools of government, after the flurry of interest of the last few years has passed. In this book, the agenda and practice of behavioural public policy have been reviewed in a balanced way, taking account of both strengths and weaknesses. In spite of taking on board the antecedents of this intellectual programme in the work of an earlier generation of public policy scholars and psychologists, for example the work of psychologists in areas such as health interventions and transport, and research on social marketing, the claim is that the strides made in behavioural economics are genuinely new because they are based on an empirical programme that modifies simple rational actor approaches. Behavioural economics was founded on identifying precise psychological mechanisms involved with human decisions, in a way that appealed to formal reasoning, and testing them in experiments and by other advanced empirical methods. It was the closeness of the founders of behavioural economics to the concerns of economists about the nature of decision-making that was the source of the salience of the intellectual programme. It kept the link to the overall aim of building a system of decision-making, which could (in time) be based on micro-foundations, and helped the programme maintain its realism and cogency.

It is no surprise to discover that once these ideas were tested they started to transform public policy. It is also consistent with the novelty of the programme that the way these ideas proved to be so acceptable was through the diffusion processes of translation, simplification, and advocacy. Skilled advocates managed to diffuse these ideas through the academy and into the think tank world, and then the ideas were picked up by elite newspapers such as the *New York Times* and the *Financial Times*. The promotion of behavioural public policy by units such as the Behavioural Insights Team was helped by this developing public agenda.

With these developments, there has been proof that these innovations work when applied by central government and its agencies. Policies have diffused across jurisdictions and levels of government, from the European Union to Australian state governments. The benefit is a more curious form of public administration based in trying things out and the regular use of rigorous evidence. Naturally, the pattern of adoption is patchy and reliant on politics rather than reflecting a uniform adoption. Not everything works either, but trials allow for easy testing and, if need be, the rejection of ideas as well as their acceptance. The process has a high degree of agency in terms of who adopts nudges and how they are implemented, rather than policy-makers being driven by the experts. As the argument in Chapter 7 shows, there are relatively few ethical constraints on the use of current kinds of nudges, except where they cause harm and deception cannot be justified. Nudges compare well with other policy instruments in standards of openness, review, and democratic justification. If nudges fail on ethical grounds, then most democratically-agreed policies would probably not pass muster either.

One approach to the current wave of reforms is to accept normalisation and good practice. In this sense, some versions of behavioural insights might be adopted as part of all policies to a degree and form part of the research support for government. This is the natural pattern of innovation. The early days were of specialist units and waves of experts. These units may no longer be needed so much if everyone practises behavioural public policy. In answer to the question of the book, nudging could be more embedded in organisational processes and be part of general policy-making. Part of this normalisation entails that nudges are used less directly and appear more generally as part of policy design. What is happening now shows a natural maturation point for nudge. The question then becomes whether a more maximal version of nudge could be adopted, which could increase the pace of innovation as well as yielding the benefits of the gradual roll-out of behavioural public policy and its greater use by public agencies.

A MORE RADICAL APPROACH

An alternative approach reflects the argument for nudge plus as set out in Chapter 8. Undeveloped in current nudges is a more reflective component, which relates to the complexities of the policy problems that citizens are being asked to help solve. Making the information component more available is one of the ways forward, in successive nudging that sometimes asks for reflection. The danger here is that there is not enough time for citizens to consider complex policy issues in the course of receiving a message, and citizens will jump to the wrong conclusions. The response to this argument is that coming to either right or wrong conclusions is what being a citizen is all about, and it is hard anyway saying what right or wrong conclusions actually are in the first place. What is important is that some reasoning has taken place, which in any case can be part of a longer journey. The wider constituency covered in nudge interventions is well worth it when compared to the limited participation of citizens in more deliberative exercises. The survey and experimental evidence appears to show that citizens prefer nudges when they are conveyed more overtly rather than covertly (Jung and Mellers 2016). Moreover, there is potential to make nudges more sensitive to citizen context by paying greater attention to the heterogeneity of impacts, such as from personalising the nudges according to known personality types. New technology, which is rolled out as part of e-government, could provide an easier way of achieving this objective by linking up databases, though some may find this moves the state to a more manipulative strategy.

The other main change is to expand the use and range of nudges being tested beyond the remit of central nudge units or even behaviouralists working in central government departments. There is a considerable local potential from nudge in the range of organisations that work in the locality and have to face the delivery issues in public policy that nudge policies are so good at addressing. There is a real issue of external validity with the use of behavioural insights in that it is not known for sure whether tests of interventions in one place generalise to another to the same degree. It is possible to get around such a limitation if national studies cover populations and have large sample sizes so as to assess the impacts of treatments in local areas, but most empirical studies are in fact not that large. There is no substitute for studies that are commissioned by organisations that have contextual knowledge about conditions in the locality.

It is often the case that local organisations are part of a delivery process involving many organisations, which involve understanding the links in the chain. Behavioural insights have been mainly used for one-off improvements to delivery, either of standard procedures or of new programmes, but there have been few behavioural evaluations in the round where each link in the implementation chain has been assessed, and where behavioural insights, as opposed to command-and-control, or incentives, have been found more likely to work. Most of all, the potential is for citizens and community groups to use behavioural insights for their own ends, whether lobbying or seeking to control their elected representatives or bureaucrats. The diffusion of new technology can make using such techniques all the easier. In these ways, behavioural insights could be used much more than they have been so far. The first wave of influence reflected the pragmatic way in which new ideas met the concerns of policy-makers; the second-wave programme can build on these achievements in a more citizen-controlled and reflective way.

References

Adams, Jean, Oliver Mytton, Martin White and Pablo Monsivais (2016), 'Why are some population interventions for diet and obesity more equitable and effective than others? The role of individual agency', *PLoS Med*, **13** (4), e1001990.

Ainslie, George (1975), 'Specious reward: A behavioral theory of impulsiveness and impulsive control', *Psychological Bulletin*, **82** (4), 463–496.

Ainslie, George (1991), 'Derivation of "rational" economic behavior from hyperbolic discount curves', *American Economic Review*, **81**, 134–140.

Ajzen, Icek (1985), 'From intentions to actions: A theory of planned behaviour', in Julius Kuhl and Jürgen Beckman (eds), *Action-Control: From Cognition to Behaviour*, Heidelberg: Springer, pp. 11–39.

Akerlof, George (2002), 'Behavioral macroeconomics and macroeconomic behavior', *American Economic Review*, **92** (3), 411–433.

Alemanno, Alberto and Anne-Lise Sibony (eds) (2015), *Nudge and the Law*, London: Bloomsbury.

Allison, Graham T. (1971), *Essence of Decision: Explaining the Cuban Missile Crisis*, New York: HarperCollins.

Altman, Daniel (2002), 'A Nobel that bridges economics and psychology', *New York Times*, 10 October.

Anderson, Joel H. (2010), 'Review of Thaler and Sunstein, "Nudge: Improving Decisions about Health, Wealth, and Happiness"', *Economics and Philosophy*, **26**, 369–406.

Anderson, Joel H. (2016), 'Structured nonprocrastination: Scaffolding efforts to resist the temptation to reconstrue unwarranted delay,' in Fuschia M. Sirois and Timothy A. Pychyl (eds), *Procrastination, Health, and Well-Being*, San Diego, CA: Academic Press, pp. 43–63.

Annis, Helen M., Howard D. Cappell, Frederick B. Glaser, Michael S. Goodstadt and Lynn T. Kozlowski (1990), *Research Advances in Alcohol and Drug Problems*, Vol. 10, Berlin: Springer.

Argyris, Chris (1993), *Knowledge for Action: A Guide to Overcoming Barriers to Organizational Change*, joint publication in the Jossey-Bass management series and the Jossey-Bass social and behavioral science series, 1st edn, San Francisco, CA: Jossey-Bass.

Ariely, Dan (2015), *Irrationally Yours: On Missing Socks, Pickup Lines, and Other Existential Puzzles*, New York: HarperCollins.

Baicker, Katherine, Sendhil Mullainathan and Joshua Schwartzstein (2015), 'Behavioral hazard in health insurance', *Quarterly Journal of Economics*, **130** (4), 1623–1667.

Bambra, Clare, Matt Egan, Sian Thomas, Mark Petticrew and Margaret Whitehead (2007), 'The psychosocial and health effects of workplace reorganisation. 2. A systematic review of task restructuring interventions', *Journal of Epidemiology and Community Health*, **61**, 1028–1037.

Banerjee, Abhijit V. and Esther Duflo (2014), 'The experimental approach to development economics', in Dawn Langan Teele (ed.), *Field Experiments and Their Critics: The Uses and Abuses of Experimentation in the Social Sciences*, New Haven, CT: Yale University Press, pp. 78–114.

Baumgartner, Frank R. and Bryan D. Jones (1993), *Agendas and Instability in American Politics*, Chicago, IL: University of Chicago Press.

Becker, Gary S. (1968), 'Crime and punishment: An economic approach', *Journal of Political Economy*, **76**, 169–217.

Behavioural Insights Team (2012), *Fraud, Error and Debt: Behavioural Insights Team Paper*, London: Cabinet Office.

Behavioural Insights Team (2015), *The Behavioural Insights Team Update Report 2013–2015*, London: Behavioural Insights Team.

Bell, Chris (2013), 'Inside the Coalition's controversial "Nudge Unit"', *Telegraph*, 11 February.

Benartzi, Shlomo (2012), *Save More Tomorrow: Practical Behavioral Finance Solutions to Improve 401(k) Plans*, New York: Portfolio.

Benartzi, Shlomo and Richard H. Thaler (2013), 'Behavioral economics and the retirement savings crisis', *Science*, **339**, 1152–1153.

Benjamin, Alison (2013), 'David Halpern: We try to avoid legislation and ordering', *Guardian*, 5 February.

Berns, Gregory S., David Laibson and George Loewenstein (2007), 'Intertemporal choice – toward an integrative framework', *Trends in Cognitive Sciences*, **11**, 482–488.

Blattman, Christopher, Julian C. Jamison and Margaret Sheridan (2017), 'Reducing crime and violence: Experimental evidence on cognitive behavioral therapy in Liberia', *American Economic Review*, **107** (4), 1165–1206.

Blume, Toby and Peter John (2014), *Using Nudges to Increase Council Tax Collection: Testing the Effects through a Randomized Controlled Trial*, London: Lambeth London Borough Council.

Borins, Stanford (2002), 'Leadership and innovation in the public sector', *Leadership and Organization Development Journal*, **23** (8), 467–476.

Bovens, Luc (2009), 'The ethics of nudge', in Till Grüne-Yanoff and Sven Ove Hansson (eds), *Preference Change: Approaches from Philosophy, Economics and Psychology*, Berlin: Springer Science and Business Media.

Bovens, Mark, Paul 't Hart and B. Guy Peters (2001), *Success and Failure in Public Governance: A Comparative Analysis*, New Horizons in Public Policy, Cheltenham, UK and Northampton, MA, USA: Edward Elgar Publishing.

Bowles, Samuel (2016), *The Moral Economy: Why Good Incentives Are No Substitutes for Good Citizens*, New Haven, CT: Yale University Press.

Branca, Francesco, Haik Nikogosian and Tim Lobstein (eds) (2007), *The Challenge of Obesity in the WHO European Region and the Strategies for Response*, Copenhagen: World Health Organization, Regional Office for Europe.

Braybrooke, David and Charles E. Lindblom (1963), *A Strategy of Decision: Policy Evaluation as a Social Process*, Glencoe, IL: Free Press.

Brehm, Jack W. (1966), *A Theory of Psychological Reactance*, New York: Academic Press.

Brehm, Sharon S. and Jack W. Brehm (1981), *Psychological Reactance: A Theory of Freedom and Control*, New York: Academic Press.

Brest, Paul (2013), '*Quis custodiet ipsos custodes*? Debiasing the policy makers themselves', in Eldar Shafir (ed.), *The Behavioral Foundations of Public Policy*, Princeton, NJ: Princeton University Press, pp. 481–493.

Broockman, David and Joshua Kalla (2016), 'Durably reducing transphobia: A field experiment on door-to-door canvassing', *Science*, **352** (6282), 220–224.

Brook Lyndhurst (2006), *Triggering Widespread Adoption of Sustainable Behaviour*, Behaviour Change: A Series of Practical Guides for Policy-Makers and Practitioners No. 4, London: Defra.

Bruns, Hendrik, Elena Kantorowicz-Reznichenko, Katharina Klement, Marijane Luistro Jonsson and Bilel Rahali (2016), *Can Nudges Be Transparent and Yet Effective?*, WiSo-HH Working Paper Series No. 33, https://ssrn.com/abstract=2816227 (accessed 12 June 2017).

Burch, Martin and Ian Holliday (1996), *The British Cabinet System*, London: Prentice-Hall.

Burd, Hannah (2016), 'Five factors for supporting people to take a more active role in health and wellbeing', Behavioural Insights Team blog, http://www.behaviouralinsights.co.uk/health/five-factors-for-supporting-people-to-take-a-more-active-role-in-health-and-wellbeing/ (accessed 19 June 2017).

Cabinet Office and Charitable Aid Foundation (2013), *Applying Behavioural Insights to Charitable Giving*, London: Cabinet Office, https://www.gov.uk/government/publications/applying-behavioural-insights-to-charitable-giving (accessed 12 June 2017).

Cabinet Office – Prime Minister's Strategy Unit (2004), *Personal Responsibility and Changing Behaviour: The State of Knowledge and Its Implications for Public Policy*, London: Cabinet Office.

Camerer, Colin F. (2003), *Behavioral Game Theory: Experiments in Strategic Interaction*, Roundtable Series in Behavioral Economics, Princeton, NJ: Princeton University Press.

Camerer, Colin, Samuel Issacharoff, George Loewenstein and Ted O'Donoghue (2003), 'Regulation for conservatives: Behavioral economics and the case for "asymmetric paternalism"', *University of Pennsylvania Law Review*, **151**, 1211–1254.

Caplan, Nathan S. (1975), *The Use of Social Science Knowledge in Policy Decisions at the National Level: A Report to Respondents*, Ann Arbor: Institute for Social Research, University of Michigan.

Caplan, Nathan S. (1979), 'The two-communities theory and knowledge utilization', *American Behavioral Scientist*, **22** (3), 459–470.

Carey, Nessa (2011), *The Epigenetics Revolution: How Modern Biology Is Rewriting Our Understanding of Genetics*, London: Icon Books.

Cartwright, Edward (2011), *Behavioral Economics*, London: Routledge.

Chabris, Christopher and Daniel Simons (2010), *The Invisible Gorilla: And Other Ways Our Intuition Deceives Us*, London: HarperCollins.

Chater, Nick, Mike Oaksford, Ramin Nakisa and Martin Redington (2003), 'Fast, frugal, and rational: How rational norms explain behaviour', *Organizational Behavior and Human Decision Processes*, **90**, 63–86.

Chen, Frances S., Julia A. Minson, Maren Schöne and Markus Heinrichs (2013), 'In the eye of the beholder: Eye contact increases resistance to persuasion', *Psychological Science*, **24**, 2254–2261.

Chetty, Raj and Emmanuel Saez (2013), 'Teaching the tax code: Earnings responses to an experiment with EITC recipients', *American Economic Journal: Applied Economics*, **5** (1), 1–31.

Chetty, Raj, Adam Looney and Kory Kroft (2009), 'Salience and taxation: Theory and evidence', *American Economic Review*, **99** (4), 1145–1177.

Cialdini, Robert B. (2009), *Influence: The Psychology of Persuasion*, London: HarperCollins.

Cialdini, Robert B., Raymond R. Reno and Carl A. Kallgren (1990), 'A focus theory of normative conduct: Recycling the concept of norms to reduce littering in public places', *Journal of Personality and Social Psychology*, **58** (6), 1015–1026.

Coelho, Miguel and Vigyan Ratnoo with Sebastian Dellepiane (2015), *Political Economy of Policy Failure and Institutional Reform*, London: Institute for Government.

Conly, Sarah (2013), *Against Autonomy: Justifying Coercive Paternalism*, Cambridge: Cambridge University Press.

Dalton, Russell J. (2005), 'The social transformation of trust in government', *International Review of Sociology*, **15**, 133–154.

Darton, Andrew (2008), *Reference Report: An Overview of Behaviour Change Models and Their Uses*, London: Government Social Research.

Davis, Rachel, Rona Campbell, Zoe Hildon, Lorna Hobbs and Susan Michie (2014), 'Theories of behaviour and behaviour change across the social and behavioural sciences: A scoping review', *Health Psychology Review*, **9** (3), 323–344.

Defra (2008), *A Framework for Pro-environmental Behaviours*, London: Department for Environment, Food and Rural Affairs.

DellaVigna, Stefano (2009), 'Psychology and economics: Evidence from the field', *Journal of Economic Literature*, **47** (2), 315–372.

Demeritt, Allison and Karla Hoff (2015), *'Small Miracles' – Behavioral Insights to Improve Development Policy: World Development Report 2015*, Washington, DC: World Bank, http://documents.worldbank.org/curated/en/505731468127152574/pdf/WPS7197.pdf.

Denford, Sarah, Charles Abraham, Jane Rebecca Smith, Sarah Morgan-Trimmer, Jenny Lloyd and Katrina Wyatt (2016), 'Intervention design and evaluation: Behaviour change imperatives', in Fiona Spotswood (ed.), *Beyond Behaviour Change*, Bristol: Policy Press, pp. 49–70.

Department for Business, Innovation and Skills and Cabinet Office (2014), *Growth Vouchers Trial Protocol*, London: Department for Business and Skills and Cabinet Office, http://www.behavioural insights.co.uk/wp-content/uploads/2015/07/bis-14-561-growth-vouchers-programme-trial-protocol.pdf (accessed 12 June 2017).

Department of Energy and Climate Change (2013), *Removing the Hassle Factor Associated with Loft Insulation: Results of a Behavioural Trial*, London: Department of Energy and Climate Change, https://www.gov.uk/government/uploads/system/uploads/attachment_data/file/236858/DECC_loft_clearance_trial_report_final.pdf (accessed 12 June 2017).

Dobson, Andrew (2011), *Sustainability Citizenship*, Weymouth: Green House.

Dolan, Paul and Matteo M. Galizzi (2015), 'Like ripples on a pond: Behavioral spillovers and their implications for research and policy', *Journal of Economic Psychology*, **47**, 1–16.

Dolan, Paul, Michael Hallsworth, David Halpern, Dominic King, Robert Metcalfe and Ivo Vlaev (2012), 'Influencing behaviour: The MIND-SPACE way', *Journal of Economic Psychology*, **33**, 264–277.

Dowding, Keith and Desmond King (eds) (1995), *Preferences, Institutions, and Rational Choice*, Oxford: Clarendon.

Downs, Anthony (1957), *An Economic Theory of Democracy*, New York: Harper.

Dryzek, John S. (2000), *Deliberative Democracy and Beyond: Liberals, Critics, Contestations*, Oxford: Oxford University Press.

Dubner, Stephen J. (2016), 'The White House gets into the nudge business', *Freakonomics Radio*, http://freakonomics.com/podcast/white-house-gets-nudge-business/.

Duckworth, Angela L., Christopher Peterson, Michael D. Matthews and Dennis R. Kelly (2007), 'Grit: Perseverance and passion for long-term goals', *Journal of Personality and Social Psychology*, **92** (6), 1087–1110.

Dunleavy, Patrick (1995), 'Policy disasters: Explaining the UK's record', *Public Policy and Administration*, **10** (2), 52–70.

Dunsire, Andrew (1993), *Manipulating Social Tensions: Collibration as an Alternative Mode of Government Intervention*, Discussion Paper No. 93/7, Köln: Max-Planck-Institut für Gesellschaftsforschung.

Dworkin, Gerald (1988), 'Paternalism: Some second thoughts', in *The Theory and Practice of Autonomy*, New York: Cambridge University Press, pp. 121–129.

Eisenstein, Hester (1991), *Gender Shock: Practising Feminism on Two Continents*, Sydney: Allen & Unwin.

Ekelund, Ulf, Jostein Steene-Johannessen, Wendy J. Brown, Morten Wang Fagerland, Neville Owen, Kenneth E. Powell, Adrian Bauman and I-Min Lee (2016), 'Does physical activity attenuate, or even eliminate, the detrimental association of sitting time with mortality? A harmonised meta-analysis of data from more than 1 million men and women', *Lancet*, Physical Activity Series 2 Executive Committee, Sedentary Behaviour Working Group, http://dx.doi.org/10.1016/S0140-6736(16)30370-1.

Engber, Daniel (2016), 'The irony effect: How the scientist who founded the science of mistakes ended up mistaken', *Slate*, 21 December, http://www.slate.com/articles/health_and_science/science/2016/12/kahneman_and_tversky_researched_the_science_of_error_and_still_made_errors.html (accessed 29 December 2016).

Engelen, Lina, Haryana M. Dhillon, Josephine Y. Chau, D. Hespe and A.E. Bauman (2016), 'Do active design buildings change health behaviour and workplace perceptions?', *Occupational Medicine*, **66** (5), 408–411.

Farrell, Henry and Cosma Shalizi (2011), '"Nudge" policies are another name for coercion', *New Scientist*, **2837**, 2 November.

Feitsma, Joram and Thomas Schillemans (2016), 'Behaviour experts in Dutch government: From newcomers to professionals?', unpublished paper.

Felsen, Gidon, Noah Castelo and Peter B. Reiner (2013), 'Decisional enhancement and autonomy: Public attitudes towards overt and covert nudges', *Judgment and Decision Making*, **8** (3), 202–213.

Fieldhouse, Ed, Dave Cutts, Paul Widdop and Peter John (2013), 'Do impersonal mobilisation methods work? Evidence from a nationwide Get-Out-the-Vote experiment in England', *Electoral Studies*, **32**, 113–123.

Fieldhouse, Ed, Dave Cutts, Peter John and Paul Widdop (2014), 'When context matters: Assessing geographical heterogeneity of Get-Out-the-Vote treatment effects using a population based field experiment', *Political Behavior*, **36**, 77–97.

Fishbein, Martin and Icek Ajzen (1975), *Belief, Attitude, Intention, and Behaviour: An Introduction to Theory and Research*, Reading, MA: Addison-Wesley Publishing.

Fiskin, James (1995), *The Voice of the People: Public Opinion and Democracy*, New Haven, CT: Yale University Press.

Flinders, Matthew (2013), 'The tyranny of relevance and the art of translation', *Political Studies Review*, **11** (2), 149–167.

Frey, Bruno S., Matthias Benz and Alois Stutzer (2004), 'Introducing procedural utility: Not only what, but also how matters', *Journal of Institutional and Theoretical Economics*, **160**, 377–401.

Fung, Archon (2006), *Empowered Participation: Reinventing Urban Democracy*, Princeton, NJ: Princeton University Press.

Gabaix, Xavier (2016), 'A behavioral new Keynesian model', unpublished paper, http://pages.stern.nyu.edu/~xgabaix/papers/brNK.pdf (accessed 14 January 2017).

Gardner, Frances and Daniel S. Shaw (2008), 'Behavioral problems of infancy and preschool children (0–5)', in Michael Rutter, Dorothy V.M. Bishop, Daniel S. Pine, Stephen Scott, Jim Stevenson, Eric Taylor and Anita Thapar (eds), *Rutter's Child and Adolescent Psychiatry*, 5th edn, Oxford: Blackwell, pp. 882–893.

Gerber, Alan S. and Donald P. Green (2012), *Field Experiments: Design, Analysis, and Interpretation*, New York: William Norton.

Gerber, Alan S., Donald P. Green and Christopher W. Larimer (2008), 'Social pressure and voter turnout: Evidence from a large-scale field experiment', *American Political Science Review*, **102** (1), 33–48.

Gigerenzer, Gerd (2003), *Reckoning with Risk: Learning to Live with Uncertainty*, London: Penguin.

Gigerenzer, Gerd and Henry Brighton (2009), 'Homo heuristicus: Why biased minds make better inferences', *Topics in Cognitive Science*, **1**, 107–143.

Gneezy, Urim and John A. List (2006), 'Putting behavioral economics to work: Testing for gift exchange in labor markets using field experiments', *Econometrica*, **74** (5), 1365–1384.

Gneezy, Urim and John A. List (2013), *The Why Axis: Hidden Motives and the Undiscovered Economics of Everyday Life*, New York: Public Affairs/HarperCollins.

Goldacre, Ben (2008), *Bad Science*, London: Fourth Estate.

Goldstein, Noah J., Robert B. Cialdini and Vladas Griskevicius (2008), 'A room with a viewpoint: Using social norms to motivate environmental conservation in hotels', *Journal of Consumer Research*, **35**, 472–482.

Gollwitzer, Peter M. (1999), 'Implementation intentions: Strong effects of simple plans', *American Psychologist*, **54**, 493–503.

Goodin, Robert E. (1982), *Political Theory and Public Policy*, Chicago, IL: University of Chicago Press.

Goodwin, Tom (2012), 'Why we should reject "nudge"', *Politics*, **32**, 85–92.

Graham, Erin R., Charles R. Shipan and Craig Volden (2013), 'The diffusion of policy diffusion research in political science', *British Journal of Political Science*, **43** (3), 673–701.

Green, Donald P. and Alan S. Gerber (2003), 'The underprovision of experiments in political science', *Annals of the American Academy of Political and Social Science*, **589**, 94–112.

Green, Donald P. and Alan S. Gerber (2015), *Get Out the Vote: How to Increase Voter Turnout*, Washington, DC: Brookings Institution Press.

Green, Donald P. and Ian Shapiro (1994), *Pathologies of Rational Choice Theory: A Critique of Applications in Political Science*, New Haven, CT: Yale University Press.

Grether, David M. and Charles R. Plott (1979), 'Economic theory of choice and the preference reversal phenomenon', *American Economic Review*, **69** (4), 623–638.

Grose, Christian (2010), 'Priming rationality: A theory and field experiment of participation in legislatures', paper presented at New York University–Cooperative Congressional Elective Study Experimental Political Science Conference, 5–6 February, New York.

Grose, Christian (2014), 'Field experimental work on political institutions', *Annual Review of Political Science*, **17**, 355–370.

Grüne-Yanoff, Till and Ralph Hertwig (2016), 'Nudge versus boost: How coherent are policy and theory?', *Minds and Machines*, **26**, 149–183.

Gueron, Judith M. and Howard Rolston (2013), *Fighting for Reliable Evidence*, New York: Russell Sage Foundation.

Hagman, W., D. Andersson, D. Västfjäll and G. Tinghög (2015), 'Public views on policies involving nudges', *Review of Philosophy and Psychology*, **6** (3), 439–453.

Hallsworth, Michael and Michael Sanders (2016), 'Nudge: Recent developments in behavioural science and public policy', in Fiona Spotswood (ed.), *Beyond Behaviour Change*, Bristol: Policy Press, pp. 113–134.

Hallsworth, Michael, David Halpern, Dominic King and Ivo Vlaev (2010), *MINDSPACE: Influencing Behaviour through Public Policy*, London: Cabinet Office and Institute for Government.

Hallsworth, Michael, Dan Berry, Michael Sanders, Anna Sallis, Dominic King, Ivo Vlaev and Ara Darzi (2015), 'Stating appointment costs in SMS reminders reduces missed hospital appointments: Findings from two randomized controlled trials', *PLoS ONE*, **10** (9), e0141461.

Hallsworth, Michael, John A. List, Robert D. Metcalfe and Ivo Vlaev (2017), 'The behavioralist as tax collector: Using natural field experiments to enhance tax compliance', *Journal of Public Economics*, **148**, 14–31.

Halpern, David (2015), *Inside the Nudge Unit*, London: W.H. Allen.

Halpern, David and Danielle Mason (2015), 'Radical incrementalism', *Evaluation*, **21**, 143–149.

Halpern, David, Stewart Wood and Gavin Cameron (1996), *Options for Britain: A Strategic Policy Review*, Aldershot: Dartmouth Publishing.

Harford, Tim (2005), *The Undercover Economist*, Boston, MA: Little, Brown.

Hargreaves-Heap, Shaun (2017), 'Behavioural public policy: the constitutional approach', *Behavioural Public Policy*, **1** (2), 252–265.

Harris, Christopher J. and David Laibson (2002), 'Hyperbolic discounting and consumption', in Mathias Dewatripont, Lars Peter Hansen and Stephen J. Turnovsky (eds), *Advances in Economics and Econometrics: Theory and Applications*, Vol. 1, Eighth World Congress, Cambridge: Cambridge University Press, pp. 258–298.

Haynes, Laura, Ben Goldacre and David Torgerson (2012), *Test, Learn, Adapt: Developing Public Policy with Randomised Controlled Trials*, London: Cabinet Office.

Haynes, Laura, Donald P. Green, Rory Gallagher, Peter John and David J. Torgerson (2013), 'Collection of delinquent fines: An adaptive randomized trial to assess the effectiveness of alternative text messages', *Journal of Policy Analysis and Management*, **32**, 718–730.

Heath, Joseph and Joel H. Anderson (2010), 'Procrastination and the extended will', in Chrisoula Andreou and Mark D. White (eds), *The Thief of Time: Philosophical Essays on Procrastination*, Oxford: Oxford University Press, pp. 233–252.

Heller, Sara B., Anuj K. Shah, Jonathan Guryan, Jens Ludwig, Sendhil Mullainathan and Harold A. Pollack (2017), 'Thinking, fast and slow? Some field experiments to reduce crime and dropout in Chicago', *Quarterly Journal of Economics*, **132** (1), 1–54.

Henderson, Mark (2012), *The Geek Manifesto: Why Science Matters*, London: Bantam Press.

Hertwig, Ralph (2017), 'When to consider boosting: Some rules for policymakers', *Behavioural Public Policy*, **1** (2), 143–161.

HM Treasury (2011), *The Magenta Book: Guidance for Evaluation*, London: HM Treasury, https://www.gov.uk/government/uploads/system/uploads/attachment_data/file/220542/magenta_book_combined.pdf.

Hood, Christopher and Helen Margetts (2007), *The Tools of Government in a Digital Age*, Basingstoke: Macmillan.

House of Lords (2011), *Behaviour Change*, Science and Technology Select Committee 2nd Report of Session 2010–12, London: HMSO.

Jackson, Tim (2005), *Motivating Sustainable Consumption: A Review of Evidence on Consumer Behaviour and Behavioural Change*, report to the Sustainable Development Research Network, Brighton: University of Sussex, http://www.sustainablelifestyles.ac.uk/sites/default/files/motivating_sc_final.pdf.

John, Peter (2011), *Making Policy Work*, London: Routledge.

John, Peter (2013a), 'All tools are informational now: How information and persuasion define the tools of government', *Policy and Politics*, **41** (4), 605–620.

John, Peter (2013b), 'Political science, impact and evidence', *Political Studies Review*, **11**, 168–173.

John, Peter (2013c), 'My nudge tour of Australia', http://bi.dpc.nsw.gov.au/blog/my-nudge-tour-of-australia-professor-peter-john/ (accessed 15 January 2017).

John, Peter (2014), 'Policy entrepreneurship in British government: The Behavioural Insights Team and the use of RCTs', *Public Policy and Administration*, **29** (3), 257–267.

John, Peter (2017a), *Field Experiments in Political Science and Public Policy*, New York: Routledge.

John, Peter (2017b), 'Behavioural science, randomised evaluations and the transformation of public policy: The case of the UK government', in Jessica Pykett, Rhys Jones and Mark Whitehead (eds), *Psychological Governance and Public Policy: Governing the Mind, Brain and Behaviour*, London: Routledge, pp. 136–152.

John, Peter and Toby Blume (2017), 'Nudges that promote channel shift: A randomized evaluation of messages to encourage citizens to renew benefits online', *Internet and Policy*, early view, http://onlinelibrary.wiley.com/wol1/doi/10.1002/poi3.148/full (accessed 13 June 2017).

John, Peter and Tessa Brannan (2008), 'How different are telephoning and canvassing? Results from a Get Out the Vote field experiment in the British 2005 General Election', *British Journal of Political Science*, **38**, 565–574.

John, Peter and Liz Richardson (2012), *Nudging Citizens towards Localism?*, London: British Academy.

John, Peter and Gerry Stoker (2017), 'From nudge to nudge plus: The future of behavioural policy', unpublished paper.

John, Peter, Sarah Cotterill, Alice Moseley, Liz Richardson, Graham Smith, Gerry Stoker and Corinne Wales (2011), *Nudge, Nudge, Think, Think: Experimenting with Ways to Change Civic Behaviour*, London: Bloomsbury Academic.

John, Peter, Michael Sanders and Jennifer Wang (2014), 'The use of descriptive norms in public administration: A panacea for improving citizen behaviours?', https://ssrn.com/abstract=2514536.

Johnson, Eric and Daniel Goldstein (2003), 'Do defaults save lives?', *Science*, **302**, 1338–1339.

Jones, Bryan (1995), *Reconceiving Decision-Making in Democratic Politics*, Chicago, IL: Chicago University Press.

Jones, Bryan and Frank Baumgartner (2005), *The Politics of Attention*, Chicago, IL: University of Chicago Press.

Jones, Rhys, Jessica Pykett and Mark Whitehead (2013), *Changing Behaviours: On the Rise of the Psychological State*, Cheltenham, UK and Northampton, MA, USA: Edward Elgar Publishing.

Jung, Janice Y. and Barbara A. Mellers (2016), 'American attitudes toward nudges', *Judgment and Decision Making*, **11** (1), 62–74.

Just, David R. and Brian Wansink (2009), 'Smarter lunchrooms: Using behavioral economics to improve meal selection', *Choices*, **29** (3), 1–6, www.choicesmagazine.org/magazine/article.php?article=87 (accessed 12 June 2017).

Kahn, Emily B., Leigh T. Ramsey, Ross C. Brownson, Gregory W. Heath, Elizabeth H. Howze, Kenneth E. Powell, Elaine J. Stone, Mummy W. Rajab, Phaedra Corso and the Task Force on Community Preventive Services (2002), 'The effectiveness of interventions to increase physical activity: A systematic review', *American Journal of Preventative Medicine*, **22**, 73–107.

Kahneman, Daniel (1973), *Attention and Effort*, Englewood Cliffs, NJ: Prentice-Hall.

Kahneman, Daniel (2011), *Thinking, Fast and Slow*, London: Penguin.

Kahneman, Daniel and Amos Tversky (1979), 'Prospect theory: An analysis of decision under risk', *Econometrica*, **47** (2), 263–291.

Kahneman, Daniel, Paul Slovic and Amos Tversky (1982), *Judgment under Uncertainty: Heuristics and Biases*, Cambridge: Cambridge University Press.

Kahneman, Daniel, Jack L. Knetsch and Richard H. Thaler (1990), 'Experimental tests of the endowment effect and the Coase theorem', *Journal of Political Economy*, **98** (6), 1325–1348.

Kahneman, Daniel, Jack L. Knetsch and Richard H. Thaler (1991), 'Anomalies: The endowment effect, loss aversion, and status quo bias', *Journal of Economic Perspectives*, **5** (1), 193–206.

Kelman, Steven (2005), *Unleashing Change: A Study of Organizational Renewal in Government*, Washington, DC: Brookings Institution Press.

Kimbell, Lucy (2015), *Applying Design Approaches to Policy Making: Discovering the Policy Lab*, Brighton: University of Brighton.

King, Anthony and Ivor Crewe (2013), *The Blunders of Our Governments*, London: Oneworld Publications.

Kingdon, John (1984), *Agendas, Alternatives, and Public Policies*, Boston, MA: Little, Brown.

Kotler, Philip and Gerald Zaltman (1971), 'Social marketing: An approach to planned social change', *Journal of Marketing*, **35** (3), 3–12.

Kundakovic, Marija and Ivana Jaric (2017), 'The epigenetic link between prenatal adverse environments and neurodevelopmental disorders', *Genes* (Basel), **8** (3), 104.

Leggett, Will (2014), 'The politics of behaviour change: Nudge, neoliberalism and the state', *Policy and Politics*, **42**, 3–19.

Levitt, Steven D. and Stephen J. Dubner (2005), *Freakonomics: A Rogue Economist Explores the Hidden Side of Everything*, New York: William Morrow.

Levitt, Steven D. and John A. List (2007), 'What do laboratory experiments measuring social preferences reveal about the real world?', *Journal of Economic Perspectives*, **21** (2), 153–174.

Lewis, Michael (2016), *The Undoing Project: A Friendship That Changed the World*, London: Allen Lane.

Lilley, Rachel, Mark Whitehead, Rachel Howell, Rhys Jones and Jessica Pykett (2014), *Mindfulness Behaviour Change and Engagement in Public Policy: An Evaluation*, http://www.sps.ed.ac.uk/__data/assets/pdf_file/0004/180787/MBCEPPreport.pdf (accessed 1 May 2017).

Lindblom, Charles E. (1959), 'The science of muddling through', *Public Administration Review*, **19**, 79–88.

Lindblom, Charles E. (1965), *The Intelligence of Democracy*, Glencoe, IL: Free Press.

List, John A. (2002), 'Preference reversals of a different kind: The more is less phenomenon', *American Economic Review*, **92** (5), 1636–1643.

List, John A. (2011), 'Why economists should conduct field experiments and 14 tips for pulling one off', *Journal of Economic Perspectives*, **25** (3), 3–16.

Lodge, Martin and Kai Wegrich (2016), 'The rationality paradox of nudge: Rational tools of government in a world of bounded rationality', *Law and Policy*, **38** (3), 250–267.

Loewen, Peter John, Lior Sheffer, Stuart Soroka, Stefaan Walgrave and Tamir Shaefer (2014), 'Expertise and efficacy in elite political decision making', unpublished paper, https://sites.duke.edu/2014bmp/files/2014/10/Loewen_et_al.pdf (accessed 15 January 2017).

Loewenstein, George (1987), 'Anticipation and the valuation of delayed consumption', *Economic Journal*, **97** (387), 666–684.

Loewenstein, George, Joelle Y. Friedman, Barbara McGill, Sarah Ahmad, Suzanne Linck, Stacey Sinkula, John Beshears, James J. Choi, Jonathan Kolstad, David Laibson, Brigitte C. Madrian, John A. List and Kevin G. Volpp (2013), 'Consumers' misunderstanding of health insurance', *Journal of Health Economics*, **32**, 850–862.

Loewenstein, George, Cindy Bryce, David Hagmann and Sachin Rajpal (2015), 'Warning: You are about to be nudged', *Behavioral Science and Policy*, **1** (1), 35–42.

Lunn, P. (2014), *Regulatory Policy and Behavioural Economics*, Paris: OECD Publishing.

Margetts, Helen, Peter John, Scott Hale and Taha Yasseri (2016), *Political Turbulence: How Social Media Shape Collective Action*, Princeton, NJ: Princeton University Press.

Marteau, Theresa M., David Ogilvie, Martin Roland, Marc Suhrcke and Michael P. Kelly (2011), 'Judging nudging: Can nudging improve population health?', *British Medical Journal*, **342**, 263–265.

Martin, Steve J., Noah J. Goldstein and Robert B. Cialdini (2014), *The Small Big: Small Changes That Spark Big Influence*, London: Penguin.

McConnell, Allan (2010), *Understanding Policy Success: Rethinking Public Policy*, Basingstoke: Macmillan.

Michie, Susan, Maartje M. van Stralen and Robert West (2011), 'The behaviour change wheel: A new method for characterising and designing behaviour change interventions', *Implementation Science*, **6** (42), 2–11.

Mols, Frank, S. Alexander Haslam, Jolanda Jetten and Niklas K. Steffens (2015), 'Why a nudge is not enough: A social identity critique of governance by stealth', *European Journal of Political Research*, **54** (1), 81–98.

NAO (National Audit Office) (2009), *Innovation across Central Government*, report by the Comptroller and Auditor General, HC 12 Session 2008–2009, London: HMSO.

Newell, Benjamin R., David A. Lagnado and David R. Shanks (2007), *Straight Choices: The Psychology of Decision Making*, London: Psychology Press.

Nooteboom, Bart (2000), *Learning and Innovation in Organizations and Economies*, Oxford: Oxford University Press.

Norman, Donald (1988), *The Design of Everyday Things*, New York: Basic Books.

Nozick, Robert (1974), *Anarchy, State, and Utopia*, New York: Basic Books.

Nyhan, Brendan and Jason Reifler (2010), 'When corrections fail: The persistence of political misperceptions', *Political Behavior*, **32** (2), 303–330.

Nyhan, Brendan and Jason Reifler (2015), 'The effect of fact-checking on elites: A field experiment on U.S. state legislators', *American Journal of Political Science*, **59**, 628–640.

OECD (Organisation for Economic Co-operation and Development) (2017), *Behavioural Insights and Public Policy: Lessons from Around the World*, Paris: OECD.

Oliver, Adam (ed.) (2013a), *Behavioural Public Policy*, Cambridge: Cambridge University Press.

Oliver, Adam (2013b), 'From nudging to budging: Using behavioural economics to inform public sector policy', *Journal of Social Policy*, **42** (4), 685–700.

Oliver, Adam (2017), *The Origins of Behavioural Public Policy*, Cambridge: Cambridge University Press.

Ostrom, Elinor (1990), *Governing the Commons: The Evolution of Institutions for Collective Action*, Cambridge: Cambridge University Press.

Ostrom, Elinor (1997), 'Behavioral approach to the rational choice theory of collective action: Presidential address, American Political Science Association, 1997', *American Political Science Review*, **92** (1), 1–22.

Panagopoulos, Costas (2011), 'Thank you for voting: Gratitude expression and voter mobilization', *Journal of Politics*, **73**, 707–717.

Park, Andreas and Hamid Sabourian (2011), 'Herding and contrarian behavior in financial markets', *Econometrica*, **79**, 973–1026.

Petrescu, Dragos C., Gareth J. Hollands, Dominique-Laurent Couturier, Yin-Lam Ng and Theresa M. Marteau (2016), 'Public acceptability in the UK and USA of nudging to reduce obesity: The example of reducing sugar-sweetened beverages consumption', *PLoS ONE*, **11** (6), e0155995.

Pike, Tony, Andrea Collier, Andrew Cotterill, Tim Everett, Rachel Muckle and Amy Vanstone (2010), *Understanding Behaviours in a Farming Context: Bringing Theoretical and Applied Evidence Together from across Defra and Highlighting Policy Relevance and Implications for Future Research*, Defra Agricultural Change and Environment Observatory Discussion Paper, London: Defra.

Pressman, Jeffery L. and Aaron Wildavsky (1973), *Implementation: How Great Expectations in Washington Are Dashed in Oakland*, Berkeley: University of California Press.

Rabin, Matthew (1998), 'Psychology and economics', *Journal of Economic Literature*, **36**, 11–46.

Reis, Rodrigo S., Deborah Salvo, David Ogilvie, Estelle V. Lambert, Shifalika Goenka, Ross C. Brownson and *Lancet* Physical Activity Series 2 Executive Committee (2016), 'Scaling up physical activity interventions worldwide: Stepping up to larger and smarter approaches to get people moving', *Lancet*, **388** (10051), 1337–1348.

Richardson, Liz and Peter John (2012), 'Who listens to the grass roots? A field experiment on informational lobbying in the UK', *British Journal of Politics and International Relations*, **14** (4), 595–612.

Rimfeld, Kaili, Yulia Kovas, Philip S. Dale and Robert Plomin (2016), 'True grit and genetics: Predicting academic achievement from personality', *Journal of Personality and Social Psychology*, **111** (5), 780–789.

Ritz, Adrian, Gene A. Brewer and Oliver Neumann (2016), 'Public service motivation: A systematic literature review and outlook', *Public Administration Review*, **76**, 414–426.

Rogers, Everett M. (1983), *Diffusion of Innovations*, 3rd edn, London: Collier Macmillan.

Ross, Heather (1970), 'An experimental study of the negative income tax', Ph.D. thesis, Massachusetts Institute of Technology, Department of Economics, http://hdl.handle.net/1721.1/13874 (accessed 12 June 2017).

Rothengatter, J.A. and John A. Groeger (1998), 'Traffic psychology and behaviour', *Transportation Research Part F: Traffic Psychology and Behaviour*, **1**, 1–9.

Sanders, David (2010), 'Behavioural analysis', in David Marsh and Gerry Stoker (eds), *Theory and Methods in Political Science*, 3rd edn, Basingstoke: Macmillan, pp. 23–41.

Sanders, Michael, Raj Chande and Eliza Selley (2017), *Encouraging People into University*, London: Department for Education.

Sartori, Giovanni (1970), 'Concept misformation in comparative politics', *American Political Science Review*, **64** (4), 1033–1053.

Savani, Manu (2017), 'The effectiveness of commitment devices: Field experiments on health behaviour change', Ph.D. thesis, University College London.

Schmidt, Andreas T. (2017), 'The power to nudge', *American Political Science Review*, **111** (2), 404–417.

Schwartz, Barry (2005), *The Paradox of Choice: Why More Is Less*, New York: Harper Perennial.

Sedlmeier, Peter and Gerd Gigerenzer (2001), 'Teaching Bayesian reasoning in less than two hours', *Journal of Experimental Psychology: General*, **130**, 380–400.

Segall, Marshall H. (1976), *Human Behavior and Public Policy: A Political Psychology*, New York: Pergamon Press.

Sent, Esther-Mirjam (2004), 'Behavioral economics: How psychology made its (limited) way back into economics', *History of Political Economy*, **36** (4), 735–760.

Service, Owain and Rory Gallagher (2017), *Think Small*, London: Michael O'Mara Books.

Service, Owain, Michael Hallsworth, David Halpern, Felicity Algate, Rory Gallagher, Sam Nguyen, Simon Ruda and Michael Sanders with Marcos Pelenur, Alex Gyani, Hugo Harper, Joanne Reinhard and Elspeth Kirkman (2014), *EAST: Four Simple Ways to Apply Behavioural Insights*, London: Behavioural Insights Team.

Shafir, Eldar (ed.) (2013), *The Behavioral Foundations of Public Policy*, Princeton, NJ: Princeton University Press.

Shafir, Eldar and Sendhil Mullainathan (2013), *Scarcity: Why Having Too Little Means So Much*, London: Allen Lane.

Shah, Hetan and Emma Dawney (2005), *Behavioural Economics: Seven Principles for Policy-Makers*, London: New Economics Foundation.

Shu, Lisa, Nina Mazar, Francesca Gino, Dan Ariely and Max H. Bazerman (2012), 'Signing at the beginning makes ethics salient and decreases dishonest self-reports in comparison to signing at the end', *Proceedings of the National Academy of Sciences*, **109** (38), 15197–15200.

Silva, Antonio and Peter John (2017), 'Social norms don't always work: An experiment to encourage more efficient fees collection for students', *PLoS ONE*, **2** (5), e0177354, https://doi.org/10.1371/journal.pone.0177354.

Silva, Antonio, Michael Sanders and Aisling Ni Chonaire (2016), *Does the Heart Rule the Head? Economic and Emotional Incentives for University Attendance*, London: Behavioural Insights Team.

Simon, Herbert A. (1947), *Administrative Behavior: A Study of Decision-Making Processes in Administrative Organization*, 1st edn, New York: Macmillan.

Simon, Herbert A. (1955), 'A behavioral model of rational choice', *Quarterly Journal of Economics*, **69**, 99–118.

Skinner, B.F. (1938), *The Behavior of Organisms: An Experimental Analysis*, Cambridge, MA: B.F. Skinner Foundation.

Smith, Adam ([1776] 1904), *An Inquiry into the Nature and Causes of the Wealth of Nations*, London: Methuen, http://www.econlib.org/library/Smith/smWN.html (accessed 10 June 2017).

Smith, Graham (2009), *Democratic Innovations: Designing Institutions for Citizen Participation*, Cambridge: Cambridge University Press.

Smith, Graham, Peter John and Patrick Sturgis (2013), 'Taking political engagement online: An experimental analysis of asynchronous discussion forums', *Political Studies*, **61**, 709–730.

Sousa, Joana Lourenço, Emanuele Ciriolo, Sara Rafael Almeida and Xavier Troussard (2016), *Behavioural Insights Applied to Policy: European Report 2016*, EUR 27726 EN, Luxembourg: European Commission.

Spencer, Charles and Jon Driver (2004), *Crossmodal Space and Crossmodal Attention*, Oxford: Oxford University Press.

Spotswood, Fiona (2016), 'Introduction', in Fiona Spotswood (ed.), *Beyond Behaviour Change*, Bristol: Policy Press, pp. 1–8.

Stone, Diane (1996), *Capturing the Political Imagination: Think Tanks and the Policy Process*, London: Frank Cass.

Sugden, Robert (2004), 'The opportunity criterion: Consumer sovereignty without the assumption of coherent preferences', *American Economic Review*, **94**, 1014–1033.

Sugden, Robert (2008), 'Why incoherent preferences do not justify paternalism', *Constitutional Political Economy*, **19** (3), 226–248.

Sugden, Robert (2016), 'Do people really want to be nudged towards healthy lifestyles?', *International Review of Economics*, **64** (2), 113–123.

Sunstein, Cass R. (ed.) (2000), *Behavioral Law and Economics*, Cambridge: Cambridge University Press.

Sunstein, Cass R. (2014a), *Why Nudge?*, New Haven, CT: Yale University Press.

Sunstein, Cass R. (2014b), *Simpler: The Future of Government*, New York: Simon & Schuster.

Sunstein, Cass R. (2016), *The Ethics of Influence: Government in the Age of Behavioral Science*, Cambridge: Cambridge University Press.

Sunstein, Cass R. (2017a), *Human Agency and Behavioral Economics: Nudging Fast and Slow*, Cham: Palgrave Macmillan/Springer.

Sunstein, Cass R. (2017b), 'Nudges that fail', *Behavioural Public Policy*, **1** (1), 4–25.

Sutherland, Stuart (1992), *Irrationality: Why We Don't Think Straight!*, New Brunswick, NJ: Rutgers University Press.

Tapp, Alan and Sharyn Rundle-Thiele (2016), 'Social marketing and multidisciplinary behaviour change', in Fiona Spotswood (ed.), *Beyond Behaviour Change*, Bristol: Policy Press, pp. 135–156.

Thaler, Richard (1980), 'Toward a positive theory of consumer choice', *Journal of Economic Behaviour and Organization*, **1**, 39–60.

Thaler, Richard H. (1994), *The Winner's Curse*, Princeton, NJ: Princeton University Press.

Thaler, Richard H. (1999), 'Mental accounting matters', *Journal of Behavioral Decision Making*, **12**, 183–206.

Thaler, Richard H. (2015), *Misbehaving: The Making of Behavioural Economics*, New York: Allen Lane.

Thaler, Richard H. and Shlomo Benartzi (2004), 'Save More Tomorrow: Using behavioral economics to increase employee saving', *Journal of Political Economy*, **112**, 164–187.

Thaler, Richard H. and H.M. Shefrin (1981), 'An economic theory of self-control', *Journal of Political Economy*, **89** (2), 392–406.

Thaler, Richard H. and Cass R. Sunstein (2008), *Nudge: Improving Decisions about Health, Wealth, and Happiness*, New Haven, CT: Yale University Press.

Tummers, Lars G., Asmus Leth Olsen, Sebastian Jilke and Stephan G. Grimmelikhuijsen (2016), 'Introduction to the virtual issue on behavioral public administration', *Journal of Public Administration Research and Theory*, Virtual Issue **3**, 1–3.

Tversky, Amos and Daniel Kahneman (1971), 'Belief in the law of small numbers', *Psychological Bulletin*, **76** (2), 105–110.

Tversky, Amos and Daniel Kahneman (1974), 'Judgment under uncertainty: Heuristics and biases', *Science*, **185** (4157), 1124–1131.

Tversky, Amos and Daniel Kahneman (1981), 'The framing of decisions and the psychology of choice', *Science*, **211** (4481), 453–458.

Tversky, Amos and Richard H. Thaler (1990), 'Preference reversals', *Journal of Economic Perspectives*, **4** (1), 193–205.

Uchitelle, Louis (2001), 'Following the money, but also the mind', *New York Times*, 11 February.

U.S. Department of Health and Human Services (2010), *Healthy People 2010*, conference edn, Washington, DC: U.S. Department of Health and Human Services.

Van de Vyver, Julie and Peter John (2017), 'A field experiment: Testing the potential of norms for achieving behavior change in English parishes', *Journal of Applied Social Psychology*, **47**, 347–352.

Varazzani, Chiara (2017), 'The risks of ignoring the brain', *Behavioral Science*, http://behavioralscientist.org/risks-ignoring-brain/ (accessed 28 June 2017).

Wansink, Brian (2006), *Mindless Eating: Why We Eat More Than We Think*, London: Hayhouse.

Wansink, Brian and P. Chandon (2006), 'Can "low-fat" nutrition labels lead to obesity?', *Journal of Marketing Research*, **43**, 605–617.

Ward, Hugh and Peter John (2013), 'Competitive learning in yardstick competition: Testing models of policy diffusion with performance data', *Political Science Research and Methods*, **1** (1), 3–25.

Webb, Eugene J., Donald T. Campbell, Richard D. Schwartz and Lee Sechrest (1966), *Unobtrusive Measures: Nonreactive Research in the Social Sciences*, Chicago, IL: Rand McNally.

Weiss, Carol H. (1977), 'Research for policy's sake: The enlightenment function of social research', *Policy Analysis*, **3** (4), 531–545.

Whitehead, Mark, Rhys Jones, Rachel Howell, Rachel Lilley and Jessica Pykett (2014), *Nudging All Over the World*, Swindon: Economic and Social Research Council.

Wiebe, G.D. (1951–1952), 'Merchandising commodities and citizenship on television', *Public Opinion Quarterly*, **15** (4), 679–691.

Wildavsky, Aaron (1966), 'Toward a radical incrementalism: A proposal to aid Congress in reform of the budgetary process', in *Congress: The First Branch of Government*, Washington, DC: American Enterprise Institute, pp. 115–165.

Wilkinson, T. Martin (2013), 'Nudging and manipulation', *Political Studies*, **61** (2), 341–355.

World Bank (2015), *World Development Report 2015: Mind, Society, and Behavior*, Washington, DC: World Bank.

World Health Organization (2009), *Interventions on Diet and Physical Activity: What Works*, summary report, Geneva: World Health Organization.

Zamir, Eyal and Doron Teichman (eds) (2014), *The Oxford Handbook of Behavioral Economics and the Law*, Oxford: Oxford University Press.

Index